Top Tax Savings Ideas

Top Tax Savings Ideas

A Small Business Tax Survival Kit

Thomas J. Stemmy

Entrepreneur.
Press

Editorial Director: Jere Calmes
Cover Design: Beth Hanson-Winter
Composition: CWL Publishing Enterprises, Inc., Madison, WI,
www.cwlpub.com

This publication is designed to provide accurate and authoritative information in regard to the subject matter covered. It is sold with the understanding
that the publisher is not engaged in rendering legal, accounting, or other professional services. If legal advice or other expert assistance is required, the
services of a competent professional person should be sought.
—From a Declaration of Principles jointly adopted by
a Committee of the American Bar Association and
a Committee of Publishers and Associations

ISBN 1-932156-64-X

Printed in Canada

09 08 07 06 05 04 03   10 9 8 7 6 5 4 3 2 1

Contents

Contents

Contents

Contents

Contents

Preface ‖

WHAT IS A TAX SHELTER UNDER TODAY'S NEW RULES? ARE SO-CALLED TAX shelters and loopholes still viable planning options now that massive tax reform has redesigned the rules of the game? More importantly, if any creative solutions remain, how can the small business owner know how to survive without paying a small fortune to the accountants and lawyers who know how the game is played?

This reference book provides an easy-to-read summary of the key tax planning alternatives debated by the professionals behind closed doors. It also demonstrates that the very concept of the tax shelter, as we know it, has undergone cataclysmic change for more than a decade. Most notably, the new laws have eliminated most of the "quick fixes" for the creative tax planner in business.

Your quest to conquer your ever-increasing tax burden must now take a different approach. If you plan to make it as a small business owner in this environment, you must recognize that you can no longer buy tax shelter relief or employ quick accounting solutions. Instead, you must prepare to deal with new, methodical rules of the game.

Although this book has been written in a concise, easy-to-read format, it involves the interpretation of a highly complex tax code and many tax regulations. Its contents will help you better understand the concept behind these rules and the planning options now available. If nothing else, you should at least know the right questions to ask your professional advisors.

To make the study complete, I draw on my experience as a tax practitioner, a university teacher, and a financial advisor to small businesses. I even reached back to the earliest days of my career when I first experienced the federal tax system in action. Those were the days when I served on the other side of the tax shelter fence as a fear-inspiring IRS agent!

Tom Stemmy
October 2003

Acknowledgments

I am grateful to the CPA firm of Stemmy, Tidler & Morris, P.A., whose faithful support and organizational teamwork made this work possible. Particular credit is given to Chris Morris who is recognized for his insights in helping settle discussions on the highly technical tax issues—all too often raised throughout this writing. To Lucy Bergling, Linda Sellner and Dan Callow I give my appreciation for the endless support and inspiration emanating from their respective positions as true accounting professionals.

This kind of writing would not be possible without a second opinion on the interpretations of the arcane tax code and its relationship to the small business owner in America. For this second look, the author turned to the PCA Group, a prestigious consulting firm with whom Stemmy Tidler & Morris, P.A. has long relied for assistance in specialty areas.

Serving the Baltimore/Washington Metropolitan area for many years, the PCA Group has created a niche in the business community by offering a unique, multidisciplined range of financial and technical services. Unlike most conventional accounting firms, they have developed a solid reputation with a one-step, holistic approach that addresses a wide variety of needs of small and large businesses alike.

With input from highly experienced affiliates, the PCA Group has shown how to meet, head-on, a wide variety of service areas that include financial planning, insurance services, technology consulting, not-for-profit solutions, and, even, mergers and acquisitions (for those business owners with a more profound agenda).

To the PCA Group, appreciation is extended for its support and guidance in this newest edition. And, special tribute is made to the tax manager of accounting (Melinda Boswell) for her top-quality technical skills and innovative writing contributions.

Finally, special thanks go to William H. Sager, Legal Counsel to the National Society of Public Accountants, for his perceptive ideas and insight. And to John Parker and Stanley Pickett, the most qualified "business lawyers" I have known during my years of practice, I extend my gratitude for their suggestions and commentary.

About the Author

Thomas J. Stemmy has more than 30 years of experience as a tax specialist and consultant. Starting out as a field agent for the Internal Revenue Service in Washington, D.C., he soon moved his career forward as a practicing CPA, an educator, and a widely published author. Mr. Stemmy is an active partner in the firm Stemmy, Tidler, & Morris, P.A. in Greenbelt, Maryland. In addition to his practice, he has taught federal taxation and business-related courses at the University of Maryland in College Park, Maryland.

Mr. Stemmy has authored numerous articles for professional publication. He has earned the coveted, nationally recognized Golden Quill Award from the National Society of Public Accountants. In addition, he is the author of *How to Slash the Cost, Time, and Aggravation of a Tax Audit*, published by Prentice-Hall.

Mr. Stemmy holds a bachelor's degree in economics from Villanova University and a master's degree in management science from National Graduate University (Alexandria, Virginia). He is licensed to practice as a CPA in Maryland and holds an enrolled agent (E.A.) designation that allows him to practice before the IRS at all levels.

Introduction

FOR MANY DECADES, AMERICA'S SMALL BUSINESS OWNERS HAVE FACED OVER-whelming odds against their long-term survival. Many have been quick to point the finger of blame at an oppressive tax system, which, they contend, continues to stand in the way of a profitable business operation. More specifically, it is the Internal Revenue Service that is often singled out as the one powerful agency that can most quickly break the small business owner.

The IRS, with its enormously complex tax code and its army of enforcement officers, is arguably the most prominent force you must contend with if you want to survive as a small business owner. Incidentally, the fact that you have this book—and have otherwise taken the first step toward legitimately reducing your potentially oppressive tax burden—suggests you just might be one of the survivors.

In recent times, there has been a systematic, albeit slow, attempt by lawmakers to help the "little guy" make it. The layperson may not agree with this assessment, and many will hasten to add that the ever-changing tax code today is nothing but a formulation designed to ultimately help the rich get richer. The professional advisor, on the other hand, sees a systematic thrust that has been doing the exact opposite in terms of preferential treatment. With one tax reform after another, you will see a trend toward creating more new tax breaks for the "little guy" while the wealthy get cut out by an array of threshold formulas that tend to stack the cards against high earnings.

And so, the good news is, that as a small business owner, you probably have a lot to look forward to—as long as the legislative momentum continues to favor your survival. However, if you want to stay in the game, you must stay alert to the changing rules. That means you should try to keep apprised of every new loophole, tax deduction, or tax deferral that could help your cause. Above all, don't be ashamed to admit it if you are utterly in the dark as to the rules of the game. You are far from being alone. Just remember that there is an immense amount of literature and Internet data out there that can help you identify the tax benefits available to you as a small business owner. And if you don't have the time or the inclination to research this material yourself, make sure you seek out a knowledgeable accountant or tax advisor. A short consultation could prove to be one of the best investments you will ever make.

1

Get to Know the Current Tax Environment

WHEN PRESIDENT GEORGE W. BUSH SIGNED THE ECONOMIC GROWTH and Tax Relief Reconciliation Act, a nation of taxpayers saw the reinforcement of a tax policy that surprised no one. Flirtations with a simplified "flat tax" scenario had been sounding good, at least in theory. But who really thought that our political forces would have created a tax code that would promote the notion that everyone should pay at exactly the same rate? In this age of complete fairness and equality for all, there exists a relentless undercurrent that demands "the more you make, the more you pay."

Whether you are for or against a policy that provides for a fair, flat, across-the-board tax rate, you may as well resign yourself to the fact that you won't see it any time soon. The new tax laws signed by the president send a clear message that progressive tax rates are here to stay.

This chapter will focus on the provisions of the current, progressive tax structure and the impact that it has on small business owners. It also discusses the recent capital gains tax revisions and how these changes will affect your tax bracket. The main objective is to highlight the tax saving oppor-

> **D**on't expect a quick fix in your business with a simple, one-line, flat tax plan anytime soon.

very smart investor or business owner should know his or her own tax bracket. Do you know yours? See tax rate schedule at the end of this chapter.

tunities in light of the marginal tax brackets that affect each and every one of us. Finally, you will learn how to deal effectively with the IRS should a problem arise.

Do You Know Your Own Tax Bracket?

It is interesting to note how few individuals have a real grasp of how much income tax they pay during the course of a year. In a recent seminar of aspiring entrepreneurs, the participants were asked to comment on their own personal income tax situation. The surprising response made it immediately clear that many had no idea how much in taxes they paid last year or how much they expected to pay at the end of the current year. And worse, the vast majority did not even have a clue as to their own personal income tax bracket. For any meaningful tax planning, you must be aware of your current and expected income tax bracket.

Individual Tax Rates Grow as Earnings Increase

Whether you operate as a corporation, a partnership, a limited liability company (LLC), or a sole proprietorship, you must plan on taking your profit out of the business sometime. This means that any change in individual tax rates will be crucial as you try to keep your tax bill down. Although the new tax acts started to phase in some modest rate reductions, higher earners still pay the most by far, with the top 25 percent of earners paying more than 80 percent of the taxes (see income-splitting strategies in Chapter 13).

Watch Out for Those Tax Bracket Cutoffs

Many taxpayers are surprised by the difference between the higher and lower brackets. Although the threshold for being taxed at these higher rates has been increased for inflation, the rates for many can still be brutal.

For example, in the worst-case scenario, in 2003 you could be taxed as high as 35 percent, a top rate that will stay in effect until 2010.

You will have reached the threshold to be taxed at this highest tax bracket if your taxable income exceeded the following:

- ◆ $311,950, if you're filing as married, single, or head of household; or
- ◆ $155, 975 if you're filing as married filing separately.

Illustration 1.1

Pierre, filing as single, anticipates a taxable income in excess of $143,500 on his 2003 individual return (this is at the threshold level for the 33% bracket).

His taxable income for the following year is expected to drop to just below $100,000.

He heard news that his sole proprietorship might receive an additional fee of $10,000 in late December because of a new contract.

If the contract fee were to be deferred until January 2004, Pierre would save $500 in taxes. $10,000 would be taxed at 28% instead of 33%.

Note: Just as with the timing of income, you can reap special benefits by timing your deductions. Thus, the business owner can do better by incurring a business deduction in a year in which her tax bracket is higher.

The Corporate Tax Rates: One Reason to Incorporate

In recent years, changes have been made that affect the basic corporate tax rates. The lowest bracket of up to $50,000 remains the same at 15%. The highest bracket is at 35%. However, this top rate only applies to those larger corporations with taxable incomes in excess of $10 million. For small business, the highest rate "tops out" at 34%. For professional service corporations, however, the current rate is a flat 35%, regardless of what your income may be.

> **M**any are unaware that business profits are often taxed at a much lower rate as a regular corporation than as an individual. Compare the tax brackets.

COMPARE CORPORATE RATES WITH INDIVIDUAL RATES

Smart business owner/operators never lose sight of their top marginal tax bracket. By so doing, you plan around paying unnecessarily high rates. The key to getting the most under the current tax law is to observe the relative differences between individual and corporate rates.

You know that the top tax rate for an individual comes to 35 percent when adding on the surtax at the higher levels. At the same time, the corporate rate might be as low as 15 percent when you are at the lowest levels. This fact, as observed in Chapter 2, prompts corporate owners to have their corporation pick up at least some of the income at the lower rates. If you are not operating as a corporation, you might think about the potential advantages of forming one.

Illustration 1.2

From Illustration 1.1, assume that Pierre operates as a corporation instead of a sole proprietorship.

Further, assume that he was personally in the top 35 percent bracket as an individual for 2003. His corporation projected a $10,000 profit.

If Pierre were to let the $10,000 remain in the corporation where it would be put to work, he could save $2,000 in taxes for 2003—paying $1,500 in taxes instead of $3,500.

Capital Gains Tax Relief: Here to Stay

A capital asset is recognized by a small business owner as investment property. It includes stocks, bonds, equipment, real estate, and the actual business entity itself. If you have ever tried to sell some stock or other investment property, you may have dropped the whole idea after realizing the stifling capital gains tax makes selling a bad economic move. If you are among those who have held onto an investment for a particularly long period, you might wonder how you could ever justify paying the tax bite after inflation has already taken its toll from your profit.

> Whatever tax bracket you may be in, the capital gains tax rates are at unprecedented lows-for some as low as 5 percent.

Special Note: Although there have been attempts to increase the capital gains tax rates, the new legislation has clarified the issue. Individuals should not have to pay one cent more than 15 percent of most capital assets held for more than one year. Taxpayers in the lowest tax bracket can pay as little as 5 percent. The difference between the capital gains tax rate and the ordinary rate is significant indeed. All small business owners must be familiar with this huge difference.

A Look to the Future: A Kinder, Gentler IRS

It finally hit home that the need to shape up the IRS was long overdue. The Tax Reform Act of 1998 included a series of tax-saving benefits, many of which will be of interest to the readers of this book. The segment of the 1998 bill that favorably affects the small business owner is direct and to the point. To set the tone, the law begins by directing that the IRS change its three-tier geographic structure—national, regional, and district offices. Now, the IRS has set up operating units that serve particular groups of taxpayers. The specific groups include individuals, tax-exempt organizations, big businesses, and—you guessed it—small business owners.

For those individuals who have had the courage to invest their time, money, and resources in a small business operation in America, there are five special taxpayer advantages in the 1998 act of which you should be aware:

1. New national taxpayer advocate
2. New burden-of-proof rules
3. New rules on privileged communications with your tax advisor
4. New rules on due process on tax collection matters
5. New restrictions imposed on the IRS on supposedly unreported income

> The image of the IRS as something to be feared has now been replaced by that of a less aggressive tax agency that is ready to cooperate with small business owners in a professional manner.

Five Advantages of the 1998 Tax Reform Act

Major changes to the relationship between the IRS and taxpayers were made by Congress in the 1998 Tax Reform Act. The following sections deal with the five major advantages created by the act.

ADVANTAGE #1: NEW NATIONAL TAXPAYER ADVOCATE

In the current law, there is an expanded role for the so-called taxpayer advocate whose job is to assist taxpayers involved in a dispute with the IRS. This can prove to be a godsend for small business owners, who will now be able to receive assistance from an individual who will be given a role as a serious advocate, an independent advocate within the IRS system.

> **Special Note:** Under the new law, small business owners will find it much easier to obtain a so-called "Taxpayer Assistance Order" (Form 911). This procedure is designed to provide intervention when a small business owner is suffering, or about to suffer, a significant hardship on account of some IRS action. You can call the Taxpayer Advocate Service at 1-877-777-4778.

ADVANTAGE #2: NEW BURDEN-OF-PROOF RULES

Prior to 1998, tax professionals had long been familiar with the one-sided rule that presumed the IRS determination of tax liability was generally correct. This meant, of course, that the burden of proof was placed on the taxpayer—who had to prove that the IRS was wrong.

For IRS examinations that began after July 22, 1998, the thrust was to throw the burden of proof, on any issue or fact, back to the IRS if you

- ◆ cooperate with the IRS,
- ◆ comply with your substantiation requirements,
- ◆ introduce creditable evidence,
- ◆ maintain adequate records, and
- ◆ are an individual (not a corporation) with a net worth that doesn't exceed $7 million.

ADVANTAGE #3: PRIVILEGED COMMUNICATIONS WITH YOUR TAX ADVISOR

Under the new law, the IRS is forced to extend the attorney-client confidentiality privilege to tax advisory communications between a client (taxpayer) and any individual authorized to practice before the IRS. In general, the privilege is to be applied in any noncriminal tax proceeding before the IRS or in the federal courts. This could be a matter of importance to many small business owners who often rely on professionals such as CPAs, enrolled agents, or enrolled actuaries.

Bear in mind, this protection only applies to tax advice, not information used in tax return preparation. Also, agents have been advised to continue asking for any information they want—it is up to the taxpayer to assert this right and deny information to the IRS.

ADVANTAGE #4: DUE PROCESS ON TAX COLLECTION MATTERS

Under the current law, the IRS must follow stringent new guidelines for enforcing tax collection policy. Designed to protect the taxpayer, the new rules state that "the taxpayer has 30 days after the mailing of a notice or tax lien to demand a hearing before an appeals officer." (By the way, the officer must not have had any prior involvement with your case.)

Generally, the IRS will be required to give you 30 days' notice before levying on property, during which time you could demand a hearing.

Both of these rules can have a profoundly favorable impact on many small business owners who have been frequently and severely harmed by the aggressive policy of certain collection officers.

ADVANTAGE #5: NEW RULES ABOUT SUPPOSEDLY UNREPORTED INCOME

In the past, many small business owners were plagued by IRS officials who took it upon themselves to calculate income based on certain observations about a taxpayer's supposed financial status. The procedure relied on was the so-called "economic reality" technique. The examining agent who used this technique essentially relied on presumptions based on certain facts and circumstances observed about the taxpayer, such as lifestyle and spending habits.

Under the new law, the IRS cannot use this procedure and otherwise allege that certain income has been unreported unless it has a reasonable indication that such income is likely to exist.

Chapter Summary

Due to major tax reform, a nation of taxpayers has seen continued efforts by Congress and the president to alleviate some of middle

America's tax burden. With their numerous tax reforms, the benefits of recent acts may help aspiring entrepreneurs and encourage existing business owners. To know how these changes will affect you and how you do business, you'll first want to

◆ be aware of your own tax bracket and keep this in mind as you make any business decision,

◆ understand the new capital gains tax rates and plan your purchases and sales accordingly, and

◆ familiarize yourself with the restructuring of the IRS so you can take advantage of the friendlier and easier-to-work-with tax environment.

As you better understand where you fall into your own particular tax bracket and the overall tax impact on your business, you can get a better picture of your operating entity, be it sole proprietorship, corporation, partnership, or LLC.

Chapter 2 will introduce you to these legal forms of doing business. Check out the various IRS publications that detail your rights regarding tax return notices, examinations, and collection action at the IRS Web site, **www.irs.gov**.

Single Individuals

If Income Is	Tax Is + %		Of Amount Over
0 – $7,000	0	10%	0
$7,000 – $28,400	$700.00	15%	$7,000
$28,400 – $68,800	$3,910.00	25%	$28,400
$68,800 – $143,500	$14,010.00	28%	$68,800
$143,500 – $311,950	$34,926.00	33%	$143,500
$311,950 +	$90,514.50	35%	$311,950

Figure 1-1. Tax tables for different categories of taxpayers (continued on next page)

Head of Household

If Income Is	Tax Is + %		Of Amount Over
0 – $10,000	0	10%	0
$10,000 – $38,050	$1,000..00	15%	$10,000
$38,050 – $98,250	$3,910.00	25%	$38,050
$98,250 – $159,100	$20,257.50	28%	$98,250
$159,100 – $311,950	$37,295.50	33%	$159,100
$311,950 +	$87,736.00	35%	$311,950

Married Filing Jointly

If Income Is	Tax Is + %		Of Amount Over
0 – $14,000	0	10%	0
$10,000 – $56,800	$1,400.00	15%	$14,000
$56,800 – $114,650	$7,820.00	25%	$56,800
$114,650 – $174,700	$22,282.50	28%	$114,650
$174,700 – $311,950	$39,096.50	33%	$174,700
$311,950 +	$84,389.00	35%	$311,950

Married Filing Separately

If Income Is	Tax Is + %		Of Amount Over
0 – $7,000	0	10%	0
$7,000 – $28,400	$700.00	15%	$14,000
$28,400 – $57,325	$3,910 .00	25%	$28,400
$57,325 – $87,350	$11,141.25	28%	$57,325
$87,350 – $155,975	$19,548.25	33%	$87,350
$155,975 +	$42,194.50	35%	$155,975

Figure 1-1. Tax tables for different categories of taxpayers (continued)

2

Choose the Right Identity to Structure Your Business

YOU, LIKE EVERY NEW BUSINESS OWNER, MUST HAVE ASKED YOURSELF AT one time or another, "What kind of business entity is best suited for my particular operation?" For most entrepreneurs, the answer lies within two specific questions.

1. Legal liability. How can I get the best protection from general business liabilities that can threaten not only my business assets but my family's assets as well?

2. Tax considerations. How can I get the best tax breaks out of the business entity that I select?

It is the second question involving the search for shelter from high taxes that underscores the subject matter of this chapter and sets the overall theme for this entire book. But first take a brief look at legal liability.

You have probably considered the question of legal liability primarily because of the ominous threat that you might one day be a victim of a devastating lawsuit. Because of our litigious society, you might have been told that you should always protect your personal assets by forming a corporation whenever you start any kind of business. Perhaps you have also been told that multiple corporations, in some cases, provide further insulation for the business assets themselves. You might have been told that a limited partnership could provide shelter from liability for investors in certain situations. And, like many start-up business owners, you've probably heard some of the clamor regarding operating as an S corporation or a limited liability company (LLC). These two options have become fashionable as tax savers and should not be overlooked.

Whichever entity you have chosen or will choose, you may be wondering if you are still facing some element of risk to your assets and the assets of your family. Because this is a book about tax saving ideas, it does not analyze issues such as legal liability and exposure to lawsuits. Suffice it to say that no two business operations are identical nor are the juxtapositions of any two owners of a business operation. What may be a smart way for your competitor to do business may very well prove to be a costly mistake for you. You might find yourself spending unnecessary time, energy, and money just to provide some overkill protection when, in reality, you have nothing but a scant exposure to legal liability.

If you are left with the slightest concern about exposure to legal liability in your prospective venture, confer with an attorney who has the right kind of credentials. In short, find an attorney who specializes in matters pertaining to business.

How to Save Taxes with Your Business Entity

New business owners are quick to learn that confiscatory tax laws have a profound influence on the success or failure of all small business operations. As a small business owner, you want to get every break available under the law, and you don't want to see the results of all your hard work get eaten up by the IRS and the tough tax laws. The problem, however, is that those tax laws have become so painfully complex that new business owners automatically assume they could never make the best of their available options without conceding the strategy planning to the tax professionals. Interestingly, the tax professionals themselves are often at odds with each other as to the best tax saving options in this ever-changing environment.

In this and following chapters, you will learn the fundamental tax advantages and disadvantages that attach to each type of business entity. You will have a working knowledge of the key tax questions raised every time an entrepreneur decides to go into business.

This knowledge will equip you to play an active role in selecting the entity that best suits your own personal circumstances. At the very least, you will learn what kinds of tax shelter options are available for each type of entity when you finally sit down with your professional tax advisor. After all, you know best all the facets and idiosyncrasies of your own business operation. Additionally, you are better equipped to ensure that your personal financial planning objectives are met.

Understand the Differences Among the Entities

Before we discuss the specific tax advantages and disadvantages of the various business entities, it is important that you know some fundamental tax considerations among

- ◆ sole proprietorship,
- ◆ general partnership,
- ◆ limited partnership,
- ◆ corporation, and
- ◆ limited liability company.

Before you start up your new business, learn which type of entity would be best for you taxwise.

The Sole Proprietorship

The sole proprietorship is thought of as the quickest and easiest way to set up a business operation. There are no blanket prerequisites, nor are there any specific costs in starting a sole proprietorship. There may be some minor formalities, however, that will need attention depending on your state or your jurisdiction. These formalities, which of course apply to all business entities, mean that you will probably have to

- ◆ obtain an occupancy permit for your place of business,
- ◆ secure a business license, and
- ◆ apply for a franchise or registration number for your operation. This registration number will be used by the state agency to monitor the collection of sales tax and other regulatory matters.

All of these procedures are simple and can be done without the assistance of an attorney or accountant regardless of the state in which you are doing business. Once you start a sole proprietorship, you are the sole owner. Unless you are in a community property state in which your spouse is vested with a one-half interest, you alone have full control and responsibility for the operation.

The General Partnership

Like the sole proprietorship, starting up the general partnership could be a relatively easy process. No costs or formalities are required. Wise counsel, however, will give you about a dozen reasons why you should have a detailed partnership agreement drafted whenever you put yourself on the line with any other individual. A few items that you would be best advised to spell out in writing are

- the amount of capital each partner is expected to contribute up front,
- the rights and duties of the partners,
- the method for sharing profits and losses,
- the authorization for cash withdrawals and salaries,
- the methods for resolving disputes or taking in new partners, and
- the method for dissolving the partnership should dissolution become necessary. Remember, this is often the case.

Special Note: Although a written partnership agreement is highly recommended, tens of thousands of informal partnerships are carrying on quite well even though they are based on nothing more than a handshake and a pat on the back. You might also find it interesting to note that partnerships can vary immensely in size and type of operation. One partnership might hold out its shingle as a small service company owned by two, while another boasts a ranking among national conglomerates grossing millions of dollars.

The Limited Partnership

A limited partnership is much like a general partnership except for one important fundamental difference. The limited partner is protected by law because the limited partner's legal liability in the business is generally limited to the amount of his or her investment. It enables this special type of investor to share in the partnership profits without being exposed to its debts in the event the company goes out of business. This protection exists as long as the limited partner does not play an active role in the partnership operation.

> **Key Observation:** The limited partnership is more tightly regulated than the ordinary general partnership because of the protective provisions extended to limited partner investors. The laws of each state dictate certain registration requirements, which usually include filing a certificate of limited partnership with the respective state agency. A written partnership agreement is necessary when forming a limited partnership.

The Corporation

Unlike the partnerships described above, the corporation is considered an artificially created legal entity that exists separate and apart from those individuals who created it and carry on its operations. With as little as one incorporator, a corporation can be formed by simply filing an application for a charter with the respective state. By filing this application, the incorporator will put on record facts, such as

> The corporation option: before you run off to form a corporation, talk to an expert about all the pros and cons.

- the purpose of the intended corporation,
- the names and addresses of the incorporators,
- the amount and types of capital stock the corporation will be authorized to issue, and
- the rights and privileges of the holders of each class of stock.

It is true that operating as a corporation has its share of drawbacks in certain situations. For example, as a business owner, you would be responsible for additional record keeping requirements and administrative details. More important, in some cases, operating as a corporation can create an additional tax burden. This is the last thing a business owner needs, especially in the early stages of operation.

Remember, aside from tax reasons, the most common motivation for incurring the cost of setting up a corporation is the recognition that the shareholder is not legally liable for the actions of the corporation. This is because the corporation has its own separate existence wholly apart from those who run it. However, let's examine three other reasons why the corporation proves to be an attractive vehicle for carrying on a business.

UNLIMITED LIFE

Unlike proprietorships and partnerships, the life of the corporation is not dependent on the life of a particular individual or individuals. It can continue indefinitely until it accomplishes its objective, merges with another business, or goes bankrupt. Unless stated otherwise, it could go on indefinitely.

TRANSFERABILITY OF SHARES

It is always nice to know that the ownership interest you have in a business can be readily sold, transferred, or given away to another family member. The process of divesting yourself of ownership in proprietorships and partnerships can be cumbersome and costly. Property has to be retitled, new deeds drawn, and other administrative steps taken any time the slightest change of ownership occurs. With corporations, all of the individual owners' rights and privileges are represented by the shares of stock they hold. The key to a quick and efficient transfer of ownership of the business is found on the back of each stock certificate, where there is usually a place indicated for the shareholder to endorse and sign over any shares that are to be sold or otherwise disposed of.

ABILITY TO RAISE INVESTMENT CAPITAL

It is usually much easier to attract new investors into a corporate entity because of limited liability and the easy transferability of shares. Shares of stock can be transferred directly to new investors or, when larger offerings to the public are involved, the services of brokerage firms and stock exchanges are called upon.

There are pros and cons to operating your business as a corporation as you will learn in the following two chapters. One of the biggest tax disadvantages for the ordinary C corporation is the dreaded double taxation. Many business owners opt for electing to operate their corporations under subchapter S of the Internal Code. Also known as an S corporation, this entity allows income to pass through to the individual shareholders. Chapter 4 covers the ins and outs of operating as an S corporation.

GET EXPERT ADVICE

Your best bet is to get sound legal advice regarding your decision. Before you approach your attorney or tax advisor, you may want to educate yourself regarding your operating options. One way you can learn more about operating as a corporation is to read *The Essential Corporation Handbook* by Carl R. J. Sniffen. In addition, many business owners are going the do-it-yourself incorporating route.

The Limited Liability Company (LLC): New Kid on the Block

In earlier editions of this book, the S corporation had been referred to as the logical choice for those small businesses that need to steer away from the regular corporation and its potential tax pitfalls. Increasingly, however, the LLC has been coming to the forefront as another viable alternative. This is especially the case now that much of the air is clearing within the various state laws and professional organizations that deal with LLCs. In fact, many practitioners argue that the LLC is now the preferred choice in the following situations where:

The Limited Liability Company (LLC) is fast becoming the entity of choice for many start-up business ventures.

- ◆ Legal liability protection is a primary concern
- ◆ A simplified "one-time" tax on the owners is preferred to dealing with cumbersome corporate tax liability
- ◆ The entity cannot qualify for subchapter S status.

An LLC is a hybrid entity that has the legal protections of a corporation and the ability to be taxed (one time) as a partnership. In many regards, LLCs are treated much like S corporations for tax purposes. However, there are some additional advantages over S corporations, including the following examples:

◆ The LLC usually offers more leeway for owners who wish to write off business losses in a business that relies on entity-related debt that is incurred.

◆ The LLC allows greater flexibility for the owner to take assets out of the company without incurring unplanned tax liability.

Remember to check with your lawyer or accountant about the advantages of the LLC in your particular state. Ask up front what it would cost to form a corporation versus the cost of forming an LLC. You may be surprised to learn that in some states an LLC could be established by filing a simple, one-page document, which lays out the Articles of Organization of your LLC, with the secretary of state.

Special Note: Prior to the current tax reform legislation, ordinary corporations were long thought of as one of the best ways for a small business owner to secure tax relief and advantageous perks. Tax reforms, however, have greatly diminished this advantage, and for some small business owners, the corporation can, in some cases, be a veritable tax trap.

In recent years, the IRS made planning alternatives available when it issued some unique rulings. What it did was offer certain nonincorporated businesses (with two or more individual owners) a low-cost opportunity to

◆ avoid some of the tax problems faced by regular corporations and

◆ enjoy the limited liability protection of duly qualified corporations.

Hence, the birth of the LLC. You can form an LLC for any lawful business as long as the nature of the business is not banking, insurance, and certain professional service operations. By simply filing articles of organization with the respective state agency, an LLC takes on a separate identity. Similar to a corporation, but without the tax problems of the corporation, it will be taxed like a partnership or a sole proprietorship.

Special Note: Businesses currently operating as a sole proprietorship should give serious consideration to forming a single-member LLC. This would enable the owner to secure liability protection without having to change the way he or she files tax returns.

A Look at Formal Steps in Setting Up Either LLC or Corporate Entity

As a small business owner, you will find that certain procedural steps need to be adhered to when setting up your business entity, whether you choose an LLC or a corporation. In taking these steps, common sense needs to be followed. Remember, too many shortcuts to save a few dollars now could wind up costing you dearly down the road.

For example, it is true that many LLCs have been formed by small business owners without any professional assistance whatsoever. With Internet access and progressive new regulations in most states, it doesn't seem to take much to get things up and running. You alone, however, need to evaluate what is being risked by putting off obtaining professional guidance. Many find that even a one-time consultation with an experienced lawyer and accountant could pay immense dividends in the long run. Don't hesitate to ask for a projection of costs from either of these professionals. And if you do most of the legwork on your own, don't be shy about negotiating the fee to review your work and to make recommendations.

Whether you have decided to form an LLC or a corporation, several fundamental steps that need to be taken once the entity has been set up. You must prepare to do the following:

- ◆ Demonstrate to the outside world that your business is being identified in its proper entity form. Advertising, letterhead, invoices, etc., should make it clear that the business is being held out to the public (and the IRS) in its proper legal name and form; for example, Roberts Rentals, LLC.
- ◆ Change the title of the assets being placed in the business to the LLC or the corporation.
- ◆ Open a new bank account in which you will transact all business in the name of the LLC or corporation.

- Apply for a federal and state ID number in the new entity name.

- Register to do business in your state and other (foreign) states where necessary.

Secure the required business liability, property, and workers' compensation insurance.

Chapter Summary

Before you consider starting a business, first give thought to the entity that best makes sense for your circumstances. Most important, remember the two major factors you must consider: (1) legal liability and its related costs and (2) tax considerations. Success or failure could very well depend on the time you take to explore both of these factors and secure advice regarding the multitude of questions that will arise.

One helpful way to learn about the state-specific laws and regulations that affect the business entities in your state is to obtain a copy of *SmartStart Your [State] Business.* Published by Entrepreneur Press, the books provide information about filing as a sole proprietorship, corporation, partnership, or LLC in the state of your choice. For more information on this series, contact the toll-free number listed in the front of this book.

As noted, unanswered questions remain about the long-term viability of LLCs and limited liability partnerships (LLPs). However, a recent polling among a number of practitioners tends to indicate the following:

- Too many sole proprietors are missing the boat by not taking advantages of the inexpensive protection from liability in their business by using the LLC form of business.

- If there is more than one owner of the enterprise, odds are good that the owner may be better off with an LLC rather than a corporation that could be less flexible for financing plans.

Type of Business Entity	Formation	Legal Liability for Business Debts	How Profits Are Taxed by the IRS
Sole Proprietorship	Easiest of all entities to set up and operate. May require a license or permit, depending on your state of operation.	The owner has complete unlimited personal liability.	Owners are taxed individually at their own particular tax rate—which could be as high as 35%.
General Partnership	Relatively simple to form and operate. A written partnership agreement is highly recommended.	All partners have unlimited liability.	Each partner is taxed individually at his or her own tax rate.
Limited Partnership	A bit more complex than a general partnership. States require a formal filing of a certificate of the limited part-nership. Limited partners cannot play an active role in partnership operations.	Only general partners have unlimited liability. Limited partners are protected from liability except to the extent of their investment.	All partners are taxed individually at their own tax rates.
Corporation	Most complex and, in most cases, the most costly to form and operate. A charter must be filed with the state spelling out the purpose of the corporation, the kind of stock to be issued, and the rights of the shareholders.	Shareholder-owners are protected from liability from corporate obligations, unless they agree to guarantee same for borrowing purposes.	Corporation is taxed separately at the corporate rates. Rates effectively reach a maximum of 35%. Note: S corporations are generally taxed at the individual owners' rates.

Table 2-1. **Key characteristics of each entity (continued on next page)**

Type of Business Entity	Formation	Legal Liability for Business Debts	How Profits Are Taxed by the IRS
Limited Liability Company	Relatively easy to form, however articles of organization must be filed with the state.	Owners are protected from liability from business obligations unless they personally agree to guarantee same. Limited liability statutes differ from state to state.	Individual owners are taxed like partners; that is, at their own individual tax rates.

Table 2-1. **Key characteristics of each entity (continued)**

3

Is Incorporation Right for You?

T O HELP YOU DECIDE WHETHER OR NOT INCORPORATION IS RIGHT FOR YOUR business situation, turn your focus toward the tax advantages of the ordinary corporation—also known as a subchapter C corporation under the tax code. For tax purposes, the ordinary corporation is identified as a business entity that is separate and apart from its shareholders. That is, it pays a separate corporate tax on its profits without giving regard to the financial circumstances of its shareholder-owners. On the other hand, an S corporation (listed as subchapter S of the tax code) generally pays no corporate taxes. Instead, it passes its profits and losses to its shareholder-owners just as if it were a simple partnership. (See Chapter 4 for a detailed study of the S corporation.)

As you might expect, there could be significant tax *disadvantages* for some business operators when they elect to be treated as an ordinary C corporation. In fact, it is these disadvantages that force you to know the difference between the ordinary corporation and the S corporation. The right choice between S and C status could save you considerable tax dollars in the long-run management of your business. The wrong choice could be an economic nightmare.

The question of whether or not you should incorporate your small business is an elusive one. Pick up any modern textbook or business manual for your answer and be prepared to find a dozen arguments explaining why any one of those entities described in Chapter 2 might be best for you.

Why are there no easy-to-follow guide-lines? Some authorities reason that there

The right choice between a C corporation and an S corporation could make a big difference in your tax bill.

are too many variables, making it exceedingly difficult for a small business owner to obtain a simplified set of rules. For example, when deciding whether or not you should incorporate, you might need to confer with your attorney and tax advisor about matters like

◆ federal regulations,

◆ state laws,

◆ investors' rights,

◆ legal liability, and

◆ extra costs required to form and operate a corporation.

These issues highlight some of the more important nontax matters that need to be considered when starting your business operation. When you add tax planning issues, you are suddenly overwhelmed by the vast amount of criteria that require your attention.

To decide if a corporation is right for your operation, you can begin by completely segregating the tax issues. Many argue that the tax issues have as much economic importance as all the other issues combined. Because this book is about tax planning for small businesses, the book's messages should get you well on your way.

The IRS and Its Ever-Changing Playing Field

Before identifying the specific tax advantages for doing business as a small corporation, it is important to take a brief look at the old rules. In so doing, you should gain a better sense of how the game is played on today's playing field.

In years past, the ordinary corporation was regarded as the only smart option for operating a small business, especially if you didn't want to be eaten alive by endless taxes on your earnings. Congress argued that too many loopholes existed, as it set out to attack all corporations thought to be enjoying too many privileges under the tax code. The smaller corporations, however, were the ones getting the real edge, because loose interpretations of the rules allowed escape from taxes or deferment of taxes year after year.

Accountants and lawyers would take pride in showing their small corporate clients how they could legally and systematically

- ◆ juggle business profits at will and pay taxes at a corporate rate significantly lower than individual rates,
- ◆ deduct bonuses to key shareholders by merely accruing them on the books,
- ◆ write off vast arrays of fringe benefits and perks to controlling shareholders while discriminating against other employees,
- ◆ break up a business into multiple corporations and make it possible to split the profits among lower tax bracket companies, and
- ◆ push retirement plans to the limit with few restrictions.

Then, after a series of tax reform movements, Congress finally took action. These allegedly outrageous tax advantages were destined to come to a screeching halt. With the stroke of a pen, Congress informed the small corporation owners that they would now have to share a level playing field with other nonincorporated business operators.

However, despite a series of tax law changes, several tax shelter maneuvers for the small business corporation survived. It is up to you to determine whether or not these remaining maneuvers can still save you money in this high tax atmosphere.

The Tax Advantages Available to Today's Ordinary Business Corporation: The C Corporation

If you and your attorney agree that a corporation is your best bet from a legal standpoint, your next step should be to check out the tax standpoint with your tax advisor. To do this, specifically look at all the tax advantages available to operators of ordinary corporations. The most popular tax advantages available to the ordinary corporation include the following:

- ◆ Income splitting

- Disability insurance
- Group term-life insurance
- Deduction for dividends received
- Capital gains benefits (if you were to sell shares of company stock)
- Medical insurance (an advantage that will soon disappear for ordinary corporations)
- Long-term care insurance
- Medical expense reimbursement plan

Income Splitting

The tax law hits many individuals with a tax rate as high as 35 percent. For corporations, the highest effective rate can also reach as high as 35 percent. (Refer to the current corporation tax rate schedule at the end of this chapter.) In short, the tide changes as the top individual rate can surpass a manageable corporate rate. How does this law affect you with a relatively small-sized business operation?

Your first question should be, who will actually pay those notoriously high tax rates anyway? According to the tables at the end of this chapter, if you were incorporated, your business would need to net as much as $10 million, after paying your salary, before that 35 percent corporate tax rate becomes effective. At the same time, you as an individual wouldn't be subject to the 35 percent rate in 2003 until your taxable income reaches $311,950—whether single or married.

The bottom line here is that most small business owners fall below those top (high income) rates. Thus, the best advice is to start taking a close look at the marginal rates in between. Accordingly, if yours is a moderate-sized income, like most of America's business owners, you may find that there is room to save a large amount in taxes by income splitting with your corporation. Put simply, this is done whenever you allocate your profit between two entities to take advantage of the lower tax brackets for each of those entities.

For example, suppose your small business corporation was getting ready to end its current business year with a modest profit from operations. Under the environment before tax reform, you might have drawn

Although it may not fit your current way of doing business, paying a little corporate tax now and then may benefit you.

out those earnings as a bonus to keep from paying unnecessary corporate taxes. However, in light of tax law changes you might have a different viewpoint.

Suppose your bonus was facing the 35 percent tax bite applicable to individuals. You might decide that this is the year you should elect to pay a little corporate tax, assuming you were in a lower corporate bracket.

Several years ago, an issue of *Money* magazine called attention to an increasingly popular solution for dealing with the "Biggest Tax Hike Ever" cast upon the American people. "Consider Incorporating," the author declared and proffered advice to those nonincorporated business owners who survived in this era of high taxation.[1] In one example, the author portrayed a business owner who was looking at a $25,000 profit, which was to be reinvested into the business. The author calculated that the business owner would have been left with $21,250 "if he had bitten the bullet and left the money with his corporation which would pay only a 15% tax." If the bonus were drawn after paying the highest individual rate, the owner would have ended up with only $15,100. The result speaks for itself. A $6,150 tax savings was available by using an ordinary corporation.

The best advice is to get a competent professional to help you crunch the numbers to see if, and when, income splitting is for you.

Before you take pains to begin the necessary paperwork to form an ordinary corporation, remember to look at the long term when planning your tax strategies. Don't think only of the short term as you try to beat the system by income splitting and paying those taxes at the lower corporate rates. You might need to pull some of those profits out for yourself sometime soon. When you do, you are going to wind up paying an income tax all over again—this time at the individual rates.

Special Case for Personal Service Corporations

Certain corporations are not entitled to take advantage of the lower graduated rates that start at 15 percent. Specifically, the personal service corporation is required to use a flat rate of 35 percent on all taxable income. The corporations that are in this category provide services in the fields of health, law, engineering, architecture, accounting, actuarial science, performing arts, or consulting. Also, to fit this personal service category, all the stock must be substantially held by employees, retired employees or the estates of deceased employees.

Disability Insurance

Disability insurance is another area involving business tax breaks. Here are the specifics:

♦ As with most self-employed business owners, you will find it is imperative to buy income protection for yourself because of the possibility that an accident or sickness can take you out of the operation for an extended period.

♦ As with medical insurance, disability premiums have grown to prohibitive levels.

♦ The only way that you're going to get any tax relief from your premium payments is by using an ordinary corporation.

Similar to medical benefits, there is a significant tax break for having an ordinary corporation pay the premiums for employee disability insurance plans. A full business deduction is allowed, while the employee does not pay taxes on the value of that fringe benefit. It makes no difference even if you, as the owner, are one of the employees.

Although disability insurance plans are a definite plus in every small business owner's tax planning program, there are three points that should be kept in mind.

1. Group plans typically cover no more than 60 percent of salary.

2. The disability benefits that you may one day receive as an employee will be taxable in those cases where the employer-paid premiums were not reported as income at the time of payment.

3. To take advantage of the full tax shelter benefits, you must be aware of certain discrimination rules.

Special Note: If your plan discriminates on behalf of the owners and higher-compensated employees, those individuals may be taxed on the value of the excess coverage not received by those other employees.

Health and Accident Plans That Pass the Test

Whether you have a medical insurance plan, a disability plan, or some combination of self-insurance, you must follow a few basic rules to get the full tax shelter for your costs.

Most importantly, you must have an actual plan set up for the benefit of the employees, not just the owners of the business. The key word here is *employee*, and to be an employee for these purposes you must operate as an ordinary C corporation.

It is interesting to note that the health and accident plan can cover businesses that have just one employee—even if that employee is you, the owner of the business. For example, the IRS ruled that certain medical insurance premiums paid by a corporate employer for the benefit of the one key employee were free of tax to that employee provided there was continued employment with the corporation. Again, the language in the plan addressed the benefits of *employees*—not the benefits of owners. It didn't make any difference that the one key employee was also the *only* employee in the entire business or that tax saving was the true motive.

Key Observation: Look for a different test if you have a self-insured health and accident plan. With this kind of plan, discrimination toward owner-managers will cause the benefits to be taxed at the level of those owner-employees, if tax saving is the sole or primary motive.

Be Aware of the Medical Savings Account (MSA) Option

Starting in 1997, certain small employers, including sole proprietorships, can get a deduction for contributions to a medical savings account (now called an Archer MSA). As with the health and accident plan, the employee is not required to pick up her or his share of the contribution as income. Although this new option has certain limitations and, in general, has not yet caught on in popularity, you should look at it as a possible option. Although it is still in a testing stage, there may be new developments at future dates.

Get rid of the guesswork in your plans, whether they involve medical, disability, or some form of a self-insured arrangement. To ensure the plan's workability, put it in writing and see that all your employees get a copy.

Technically, a health and accident plan does not have to be in writing, nor must it be a formal arrangement to take advantage of the plan's tax-sheltered benefits. However, if there is no written plan, be prepared to demonstrate that a plan actually exists, either by prior practice or by prior agreement to make the medical payments. (It is a good idea to document the existence of your plan in the corporate minutes.) Regardless, make sure you notify your employees about the existence of the plan.

Illustration 3.1

In a well-known tax court case, it was ruled that a plan did not exist where a corporation, without a prior history of employee reimbursement for medical costs, paid the medical expenses of a $10-per-week former employee.

The employee was the aged mother of the corporation's four shareholders.

The tax court would not accept the contention that the corporation was prepared to assist any faithful and long-term employee who suffered from a lack of funds. This arrangement, it pointed out, did not constitute an acceptable plan.

Group Term-Life Insurance

A corporate employer is still permitted to provide its employees up to $50,000 of group term-life insurance protection without a tax cost to those employees. The group term insurance must be provided under a policy carried by the corporate employer that complies with the following conditions:

◆ Provides for the benefit of a group of employees as compensation for services rendered to the corporation

◆ Does not discriminate in favor of key employees in eligibility to participate or receive benefits

Although group term-life insurance plans generally involve 10 full-time employees, there are special rules to qualify group plans for organizations with fewer than 10 employees. To qualify for the death benefit exclusion, you must show that the insurance

◆ is available for all full-time employees

and

♦ provides protection based on a uniform percentage of compensation or is set on the basis of coverage brackets set by the insurer, not the corporation.

Corporations with fewer than 10 employees will not be disqualified from the tax-shelter benefits of group term-life insurance if they do not provide coverage for

♦ part-time personnel who normally do not work more than 20 hours per week or five months in any calendar year,

♦ those employed less than six months, and

♦ employees who are 65 and found to be uninsurable based on data provided by an insurance company's questionnaire.

Deduction for Dividends Received

The deduction for dividends received is one of the most overlooked tax breaks by owners of small business corporations. If you have an ordinary C corporation that owns shares of stock in another unrelated corporation, the dividends you receive from your investment will, to a large extent, get tax-free treatment. That is, as much as 70 percent of those dividends received will be free from tax by virtue of this special deduction.

For the most part, all that is required to qualify for this deduction is to show that the dividends received were, in fact, paid by another domestic corporation that is subject to income tax. That probably includes that great stock tip recommended by your investment advisor.

Take heed to note that the special dividend deduction does not apply to the following types of dividends:

♦ Dividends from deposits on withdrawal accounts in building and loans associations, mutual savings banks, and cooperatives

♦ Capital gain dividends and returns of capital

♦ Dividends received from debt-financed stock when debt is incurred to purchase the stock

Special Note: The total amount of dividends that you may claim is generally limited to 70 percent of your corporation's taxable income.

Illustration 3.2

L ong's Home Improvement Corporation, a small family-owned and operated business, had started to accumulate some additional capital that it needed to retain for operating reserves and some possible future expansion.

Joe Long had become disenchanted with the meager interest rates being generated by the corporation's money market funds and CDs at the bank. Looking ahead to some better yields and some future growth, Joe started to invest about $15,000 each year in attractive, high-yielding stocks that touted generous dividend yields.

The corporation, over a period of time, enhanced its financial position measurably as its stock portfolio outdistanced the more conservative fixed-income investments. The real bonanza to Long's Corporation was found in the attractive cash flow being generated by those high dividend distributions that were paid by other domestic corporations. Joe found this to be 70 percent tax-free. Joe thought that his option was similar to tax-free bonds, but the investments were expected to grow in value over time.

Capital Gains Benefit: Sale of the Shares of Stock in Your Business

Many investors agree that the ultimate tax bite has for too long stifled the incentive of those who would dare to invest in a small business. A common feeling is that when the time comes for the small business owner to sell out, a confiscatory tax will be assessed. Often, when you couple the tax with a persistent inflation factor for the years in business, little remains for the entrepreneur's risk and hard work. However, some relief is available by way of special capital gains tax provisions.

The capital gains tax is a reduced tax reserved for those who sell special investment property. That special property includes certain business property, including stock in a corporation that was held for investment purposes, usually more than one year. Accordingly, when you sell your small business's stock, expect to have the capital gains rules apply to your profits.

Special Note: For those in the lowest tax bracket, the maximum capital gains tax rate can be an attractive 5 percent.

Q. How much capital gains tax will I have to pay under the new law if I sell the stock in my corporation?

A. In most cases, this tax rate is the same as the investor's marginal tax bracket; however, the maximum charge is generally 15 percent. For many years, there had been no concessions or tax benefits given by the government no matter how long you held onto your investment. Also, it should be noted that the lowered 15 percent rate is in addition to any state taxes whenever applicable.

Chapter Summary

In addition to the general tax benefits of incorporating covered in this chapter, you must understand the term *fringe benefits* as it relates to the tax law. In Chapter 6, you will receive a full explanation, including the following:

- ◆ A list of the various fringe benefits available to all business entities under the current law
- ◆ Suggestions on how those benefits can be used to your tax advantage

As a business owner who operates as an ordinary C corporation, you should take note of two specific fringe benefits whose full tax-sheltered advantage only comes about when the employer is an ordinary corporation. Those two fringe benefits detailed in Chapter 6 are medical care and meals and lodging.

You will observe that both of these special benefits involve the following two-fold tax advantage:

- ◆ The employer (the corporation) will get a full tax deduction for the benefit paid.
- ◆ The employees will be permitted to exclude that benefit from their taxable income.

A final thought on the regular C corporation: because of current IRS trends, it is the author's opinion that the regular C corporation has already lost favor as the top choice of the small business owner. With the medical insurance fringe benefit being extended to other business entities, the only real tax advantage for the C corporation will be the income-splitting option.

Over	But Not Over	The Tax Is	Of Excess Over
$0	$50,000	15%	$0
$50,000	$75,000	$7,500 + 25%	$50,000
$75,000	$100,000	$13,750 + 34%	$75,000
$100,000	$335,000	$22,250 + 39%	$100,000
$335,000	$10,000,000	$113,900 + 34%	$335,000
$10,000,000	$15,000,000	$3,400,000 + 35%	$10,000,000
$15,000,000	$18,333,333	$5,150,000 + 38%	$15,000,000
$18,333,333	—	35%	$0

Table 3-1. **2003 corporation tax rate schedule**

NOTE

1. Lohse, Deborah, "The Biggest Tax Hike Ever," *Money*, August 1993, 58-63.

4

Become Familiar with the S Corporation Alternative

AN S CORPORATION IS ONE THAT HAS ALL THE LEGAL PROTECTION AND economic benefits of an ordinary corporation. There is, however, one significant characteristic that it doesn't share—it doesn't pay taxes like the ordinary corporation. In fact, except in isolated cases, it doesn't pay any taxes at all. Thus, the S corporation is more akin to a partnership or a sole proprietorship. Accordingly, its profits and losses are passed off to its owners just as if a corporation never existed.

Since 1958, the use of the S corporation has been a valuable planning tool for the small business owner. In fact, for some time, many have considered it to be the top choice. However, in recent years it might be argued that the LLC is taking the lead. (For more details, see "The Limited Liability Company (LLC): New Kid on the Block" in Chapter 2.) This chapter will give the reasons for the popularity of the S corporation, which will benefit not only new business owners but also owners of ordinary corporations who are looking to make changes to get tax relief.

In this regard, you are reminded that a major reason for the interest in S corporation status is the disenchantment with some of the tax disadvantages that accompany the ordinary C corporation. Those disadvantages are identified throughout this chapter as you learn about the advantages of the S corporation.

When you examine the following benefits of S corporations, remember to consider the trade-offs. Try to evaluate the dollar savings that will be lost when you concede the tax benefits—medical reimbursement plans, income splitting, etc.—that are ordinarily allowed only to the C corporation. Only by observing the entire picture can you be assured of attaining the best possible tax breaks.

For information about applying for S corporation status, see the end of this chapter for forms and guidelines.

No Corporate Income Tax to Pay on Profits

No tax for S corporations? The inexperienced business owner might be puzzled over this advantage. If the corporation doesn't pay taxes, then the shareholders will be required to pay personally. In other words, a tax bill at individual rates rather than at the corporate level. Remember, it was pointed out earlier that there were distinct advantages to paying a corporate tax, at least periodically. This is because the corporate tax rate could be lower, perhaps as low as 15 percent.

In Chapter 3 you learned how the technique of income splitting enables you to move income out of the high individual brackets into the lower-tiered corporate rates. Income splitting has become especially popular in recent years because of the relatively high individual rates. So, in light of this tax shelter, why elect S status and forego the benefits of income splitting available with an ordinary corporation?

Income splitting with the ordinary corporation only makes sense when the corporate owner can afford to leave the profits in the corporation for future growth and development. If you are not in that enviable position, you need to be aware that there are certain risks when you have to pull out your profits intermittently throughout the year.

Key Observation: Income splitting is sometimes not a workable solution because many small corporation owners tend to pull out their profits in salaries and bonuses as they are earned. There is usually little, if any, corporate tax left to pay at those low marginal rates when an ordinary corporation is used.

WHAT ARE THE RISKS IN A REGULAR CORPORATION?

There is a risk because the periodic draws that you make (bonuses, fringe benefits) may not be allowed as a deduction to the corporation. While you may think that all those special draws taken from the corporation are legitimate business deductions, the government might think otherwise. As it has done so often in the past, the IRS may try to characterize those payments as nondeductible dividends.

Accordingly, you could actually be required to pay a double tax as an ordinary corporation. This is because the corporation will have to pay a tax on those profits, and you, the shareholder, will pay a tax once again on the distribution.

Special Note: The 2003 tax law reduced the maximum tax rate on most dividends to 15 percent. This change significantly softens the double tax blow.

Finally, the advantage of not having to pay corporate income taxes by choosing S status is one of simplicity in an otherwise complicated process. When you don't have to pay a corporate income tax, there is no guesswork between corporate tax rules and individual rules, not to mention the difference in the rates. There is one tax only. The corporation merely acts as a conduit and passes the income to the owners—one time only.

Avoid Reasonable Compensation Problems

As noted above, one of the constant problems facing the ordinary C corporation is the potential threat by the IRS to disallow as business deductions the salaries and bonus payments to shareholders. To protect your corporation from this costly scenario, you need to take continuing steps each year to prove the legitimacy of these payments made to you.

Many feel that it is unfair that the IRS rarely challenges the compensation paid to nonstockholders and other unrelated parties. After all, salaries and wages are supposed to be just one more category on the accepted list of *ordinary and necessary* business expenses. But when those wages are paid to a shareholder-owner, a whole different set of standards is applied.

The special standards for shareholder compensation will be explained in Chapter 5; however, for the purpose of this segment, you should be aware of the following facts:

> **B**eware: many owners of small C corporations are surprised to learn that they could be penalized for paying themselves too much salary.

♦ For the C corporation to deduct salary payments to a shareholder, a *reasonable test* must be met.

♦ You may need to prove that the amount of the salary payment was justified in view of the hours you worked, your experience, your education, and the complexity of the job.

> **Q.** Since owners of ordinary corporations have to worry about justifying their actions to the IRS every time they take money out of their businesses, is it better to switch to S status and eliminate these potential problems entirely?
>
> **A.** No, not because of this issue alone. The IRS has shown a pattern of auditing closely held corporations and challenging the amounts paid to the shareholder-owners. The courts, however, have sided more with the business owner in recent years. This implies that there has been a growing intolerance of government trying to dictate reasonable standards by telling hard-working business owners how much their services are worth.

In conclusion, the risk of having your own personal draws and special payments disallowed as business expenses still exists. You need to weigh this fact and decide if those tax sheltering benefits offered by the ordinary corporation (outlined in Chapter 3) will only lead to major tax problems down the road. Remember, as your profit margins and cash distributions increase, so does the risk of an IRS challenge to the money that you take out.

Avoid the Personal Holding Company Tax

Personal holding company tax implications can be avoided by electing S corporation status. The personal holding company tax might be called a special *penalty tax*, which is imposed on ordinary corporations that generate too much personal holding company income. Put another way, the penalty tax is imposed on those *ordinary* corporations that might be defined as "a personal holding company."

Key Observation: The prime target of this penalty tax is the so-called incorporated pocketbook, that is, a corporation that idly stands by and holds investment income for the shareholder-owners.

What is the personal holding company income that is subject to the penalty tax? In general terms, personal holding company income consists of items such as

♦ dividends, interest, royalties and annuities;

♦ rents and royalties (with certain adjustments); and

♦ amounts received for contracts for personal services if the corporation doesn't dictate who will perform the services.

Q. When will the personal holding company tax be applied?
A. This penalty is applied when personal holding company income makes up at least 60 percent of the adjusted gross income of the corporation. Also, the tax will only apply when 50 percent of the corporation's stock is owned by no more than five individuals.

You can be prepared! If it appears that your ordinary corporation is proportionately generating too much of those personal holding company income items as previously defined, pay as much money as is legitimately possible to the shareholder-employees so that no profit is left to be taxed.

Avoid the Accumulated Earnings Tax

S corporation election is, once more, another way to avoid accumulated earnings tax, a penalty tax that often catches the unwary small business owner off guard. The tax is imposed on ordinary corporations when they are deemed to have improperly accumulated income. Under this subjective test, the IRS looks over the corporate owner's shoulder and tries to decide if the corporation has been retaining too much of its profits. The insinuation is that if those profits had been properly distributed to the shareholders, an additional income tax would have been paid by those shareholders as individuals.

The rate of tax on so-called improper accumulations had long been accepted at a flat 28 percent on accumulated taxable income. As a result of the 1993 tax act, the penalty tax was raised to 39.6 percent for corporate tax years after 1992. The very thought of this "penalty" threat has long been a thorn in the sides of small corporation owners. Now, thanks to the 2003 tax act, the special tax has been reduced to a manageable 15 percent. Consult with your tax advisor about utilizing the consent dividend as a means of eliminating the potentially egregious tax liability.

The penalty tax will not apply until the accumulated earnings and profits of the corporation exceed $250,000. (For certain service corporations, the allowance is $150,000.)

If it appears that your corporation will tend to accumulate substantial profits, rather than paying them all out as you go, you should consider an election under subchapter S. An S corporation is not subject to this tough penalty tax as long as the S election is in force. Keep in mind, corporations that were formerly ordinary C corporations can still be exposed to IRS attack.

Below you will find a checklist of reasons that may, in individual cases, give justifiable reason for accumulating profits beyond the prescribed allowances.

Checklist of Acceptable Reasons to Accumulate Income in a Corporation Beyond the Prescribed Allowance

❏ Business expansion and plant replacement
❏ Acquisition of either stock or assets
❏ Payment of debts
❏ Working capital
❏ Investments or loans to customers or suppliers on whom the corporation relies for its continuing business

Special Note: It has been determined that the self-insurance of product liability risks is also a qualifying business need for which earnings and profits may be accumulated without incurring the accumulated earnings tax penalty.

Enjoy Several Loss Pass-Through Benefits

Like many start-up business owners, you might expect to lose money in the first year or so. The loss pass-through benefit is of key interest to you.

The ordinary business corporation, you will recall, is a taxable entity wholly separate from its individual shareholders. When a profit is generated, the corporation pays the applicable income taxes.

When a loss is realized, it can only be used to offset corporate profits and cannot give immediate tax benefits to the shareholder-owner.

For newly organized ordinary corporations, the losses generated must be carried forward, up to 20 years, and can be used only when taxable income occurs.

Illustration 4.1

Pat Brown, a retired engineer, invests $75,000 to form Brown Corporation, an ordinary C corporation. With his monthly retirement and income from investments, Pat is already in the highest tax bracket.

During the first start-up year, Brown Corporation incurs a loss of $30,000.

Although Pat desperately needs personal tax shelter during this period, he cannot write off one cent from the corporation loss.

The loss, instead, must be carried forward to subsequent years when, hopefully, profits will begin.

In retrospect, had Pat filed a timely election for S status, he would have been able to write off the full $30,000 on his individual tax return for that year.

In the scenario spelled out in Illustration 4.1, suppose Pat wanted to take advantage of the tax-sheltered breaks of income splitting that are available only to the ordinary C corporation. Pat also would have liked to be able to write off those heavy start-up losses in the first year of business. What should he have done?

Pat should have filed an election to be taxed as an S corporation immediately at the start of business in that first year when he knew that a loss would occur. During a later period, when it is determined that profits are to begin, a revocation of the election should be made.

Special Note: You should try to plan ahead for the year that a profit is projected and switch from S status to that of an ordinary corporation. For S status to be revoked and ordinary corporation treatment to begin during a particular taxable year, a deadline must be met. A majority of the share-holders must file a consent to terminate the election by the 15th day of the third month of the taxable year.

Remember, if that deadline is not met, the entire year will remain in S status unless an event occurs that would disqualify the corporation from continuing as an S corporation. Although these strict deadlines have been relaxed somewhat by the IRS in recent years, it is always cost efficient to try and file in a timely manner.

Avoid Double Taxation When Liquidating a Business

Perhaps the biggest cause for the recent mass exodus from ordinary corporation status to subchapter S points to a liquidation rule, which was written as part of the 1986 tax act. What that revision did was eliminate a longtime tax-shelter benefit allowed to those business owners who decided to call it quits.

What benefit was eliminated? Under the old rules, the corporation had a special privilege allowing it to exclude from income most of the gains it made when it sold out its assets in a liquidation process. The purpose was to ensure there would be one tax only when the shareholders received their final payout. Under current law, that favorable tax incentive for investing in a business has come under serious threat. Instead of a reward for investing in an ordinary C corporation, the owners will find themselves penalized with a debilitating *double tax*. For example:

> Too many corporations are operating wholly unaware that a "double tax" could blindside them if they ever sell out as a regular corporation.

- ◆ When a corporation sells off its assets, it must now pay the applicable corporate rates on the gains.
- ◆ When individual shareholders receive the payoff distribution for their stock shares, they are subject to another capital gains tax on their entire profit.

It is interesting to note that the current rule took this penalty provision a step further to make sure that no benefits remain. For example, if a corporation simply distributes property, other than cash, to its shareholders in the liquidation process, gain will *still* have to be recognized as taxable—just as if the assets had been sold by the corporation at fair market value. The following illustration demonstrates the impact of the new law on ordinary corporations.

Illustration 4.2

In 2002, Lena Roe owns all of the stock of Roe Corporation, an ordinary C corporation. Her cost basis of that stock was $10,000.

Roe Corporation has one single asset, originally purchased for $200,000.

In accordance with its liquidation plan, Roe sells the asset for $500,000 and the $500,000 proceeds are distributed to Lena.

Roe Corporation has a taxable gain of $300,000. Roe pays a tax at 34% in the amount of $102,000.

In this scenario, Lena has the following gain from the liquidation:

Amount of proceeds received	$500,000
Minus corporate tax liability	102,000
Net amount received	398,000
Minus cost basis of the stock	10,000
Gain to be reported by Lena	$388,000

The overall tax bill is:

Lena's tax at 20% ($388,000 multiplied by .20)	$77,600
The corporation's tax	102,000
The total tax bill	$179,600

Had Lena elected to file under subchapter S at the beginning, the tax bill at liquidation might be as low as:

Corporate tax:	0
Lena's tax:	
Tax on the corporate sale	$60,000
($300,000 multiplied by .20)	
Total tax	$60,000

Note: Because of the double tax provision under the current law, election to file for S corporation status might effectively save Lena $119,600 in taxes upon liquidation. Although this saving should be adjusted for prior taxes paid on S corporation earnings, the inference is clear. A double tax is a high price to pay for an ordinary C corporation.

Special Note: Because the new tax act lowered the capital gain rate to 15 percent for individuals, the double tax burden would have been reduced somewhat if the sale occurred after 2002.

Converting Your Regular Corporation to S Status

At one time or another, most small business owners operating as C corporations have considered making an S election, particularly when they grasp the potential tax savings that could be generated upon liquidation. To thwart this effort toward avoiding the double tax, the government has put up several roadblocks, and the most effective dissuasion has been the so-called "built-in gains tax."

This tax is nothing but a method for locking in the much-feared double tax the very moment that the corporation coverts to S status. It is based on a calculation that looks at the value of the corporate assets at the time of conversion and then locks in a built-in gain figure, placing it on record for future reference. Then, for a 10-year period, the specter of the double tax looks down on the operating business waiting to be triggered.

There are a number of ways to reduce, postpone, or eliminate the built-in gains tax, but without proper planning, the hit can take the business owner by surprise. Of course, the best thing to do is to avoid it altogether by making the S conversion before the business has increased its asset values, which, in turn, generates built-in gains.

Special Note: The protective election to convert to S status is not for everyone. In certain situations (particularly with cash-basis businesses), an immediate tax consequence could outweigh the long-term protection against the double tax.

Illustration 4.3

As you conclude Chapter 4 and understand the tax advantages of the S corporation, take a moment to reflect upon the business owner's need to see the whole picture. The following anecdote identifies some very typical concerns in a common scenario.

Terry prepares to start a small business with a modest amount of cash and some bank financing. Immediate profits are expected, so Terry is advised by her attorney to form a corporation, which she is told will allow her more flexibility for raising additional capital plus provide protection from personal liability.

Terry needs medical and disability insurance, but the cost is a prohibitive $8,000 annually for two policies. Terry expects to have one employee at first, but that employee is covered by outside insurance and will not come under the corporation's health and accident plan.

Terry's advisor notes a classic tax-shelter scenario regarding expected health and accident plans and other incidental fringe benefits: in her 28 percent tax bracket, Terry is advised she can pocket up to $2,240 in tax savings annually for the insurance payments alone. Under a qualified health and accident plan, all premiums paid and deducted by the corporation would be tax-free to Terry as an employee, or $8,000 multiplied by 28 percent.

Terry reacts to the newfound tax bonanza by thinking, "It looks like an ordinary corporation is the way to go." She tallies up all the tax-shelter benefits, including the minor fringe benefit allowances that would not be allowed if the S corporation alternative was elected.

She and her advisors explore the possible downsides. The accountant then explains the ordinary C corporation disadvantages. Except for some cautions about reasonable compensation, there doesn't appear to be any major risk to operate as an ordinary corporation.

But her final question to her well-educated advisors, "What happens when I sell the business?" brings a new twist to the planning scenario. Terry plans to operate and develop the business for about eight years and then sell it, projecting that it would sell for a profit in the $500,000 range.

Because of that plan and the double tax on liquidations, the final scenario is surprising.

◆ With an ordinary C corporation, the overall "double" tax on the liquidation may be close to 50 percent—or $250,000.

◆ With an S corporation, the federal tax may be as low as 15 percent—or $75,000.

In an additional sobering update, Terry is informed that the once-valuable fringe benefit for health insurance for regular corporations is being phased out and that, in short, by 2003 the changing tax law would extend full deductibility to all business owners—not only to regular corporations.

With this information, the matter is decided. Even with the relatively modest tax savings that would be enjoyed year after year, there is no plausible reason for Terry to subject herself to the double tax by operating as an ordinary corporation. The onerous penalty tax upon sale would not apply with a successful S corporation.

Your next step is to send *Form 2553, Election by a Small Business Corporation,* to the IRS to be treated as an S corporation. A sample copy of this form is located at the end of the chapter to give you an idea of what is required of you.

Special Note: In general, most domestic (U.S.) corporations with fewer than 75 shareholders and only one class of stock can be eligible for S corporation status. However, you should check with your advisor for other eligibility requirements.

Chapter Summary

The S corporation long ago became a popular vehicle for tax-planning purposes. In fact, many so-called regular corporations have been electing to switch to the S provisions in order to negate several burdensome (if not catastrophic) tax implications within the overall picture. For others, however, there are shorter-term tax benefits for operating as a regular corporation. As a small business owner, you need to know if (or when) it makes sense to consider something other than a regular corporation.

If you are already operating as a regular corporation and feel the arrangement is not serving your best interest, you may want to convert to S status (Form 2553 to be filed). On the other hand, if you're just starting your business, you should take a look at the limited liability company.

Form **2553** (Rev. December 2002) Department of the Treasury Internal Revenue Service	**Election by a Small Business Corporation** (Under section 1362 of the Internal Revenue Code) ▶ See Parts II and III on back and the separate instructions. ▶ The corporation may either send or fax this form to the IRS. See page 2 of the instructions.	OMB No. 1545-0146

Notes: 1. Do not file Form 1120S, U.S. Income Tax Return for an S Corporation, for any tax year before the year the election takes effect.
      2. This election to be an S corporation can be accepted only if all the tests are met under Who May Elect on page 1 of the instructions; all shareholders have signed the consent statement; and the exact name and address of the corporation and other required form infor mation are provided.
      3. If the corporation was in existence before the effective date of this election, see Taxes an S Corporation May Owe on page 1 of the instructions.

Part I   Election Information

Please Type or Print	Name of corporation (see instructions)	A Employer identification number
	Number, street, and room or suite no. (If a P.O. box, see instructions.)	B Date incorporated
	City or town, state, and ZIP code	C State of incorporation

D Check the applicable box(es) if the corporation, after applying for the EIN shown in A above, changed its name ☐ or address ☐
E Election is to be effective for tax year beginning (month, day, year) . . . . ▶   /   /
F Name and title of officer or legal representative who the IRS may call for more information   G Telephone number of officer or legal representative   (   )

H If this election takes effect for the first tax year the corporation exists, enter month, day, and year of the earliest of the following: (1) date the corporation first had shareholders, (2) date the corporation first had assets, or (3) date the corporation began doing business . . . . ▶   /   /

I Selected tax year: Annual return will be filed for tax year ending (month and day) ▶ . . . .
If the tax year ends on any date other than December 31, except for a 52–53-week tax year ending with reference to the month of December, you must complete Part II on the back. If the date you enter is the ending date of a 52–53-week tax year, write "52–53-week year" to the righ t of the date.

J Name and address of each shareholder; shareholder's spouse having a community property interest in the corporation's stock; and each tenant in common, joint tenant, and tenant by the entirety. (A husband and wife (and their estates) are counted as one shareholder in determining the number of shareholders without regard to the manner in which the stock is owned.)	K Shareholders' Consent Statement. Under penalties of perjury, we declare that we consent to the election of the above-named corporation to be an S corporation under section 1362(a) and that we have examined this consent statement, including accompanying schedules and statements, and to the best of our knowledge and belief, it is true, correct, and complete. We understand our consent is binding and may not be withdrawn after the corporation has made a valid election. (Shareholders sign and date below.)		L Stock owned		M Social security number or employer identification number (see instructions)	N Share-holder's tax year ends (month and day)
	Signature	Date	Number of shares	Dates acquired		

Under penalties of perjury, I declare that I have examined this election, including accompanying schedules and statements, and to the best of my knowledge and belief, it is true, correct, and complete.

Signature of officer ▶   Title ▶   Date ▶

For Paperwork Reduction Act Notice, see page 4 of the instructions.   Cat. No. 18629R   Form **2553** (Rev. 12-2002)

Figure 4-1. Form 2553, Election by a Small Business Corporation (continued on next page)

Become Familiar with the S Corporation Alternative

Part II Selection of Fiscal Tax Year   (All corporations using this part must complete item O and item P, Q, or R.)

O   Check the applicable box to indicate whether the corporation is:

   1. ☐ A new corporation adopting the tax year entered in item I, Part I.

   2. ☐ An existing corporation retaining the tax year entered in item I, Part I.

   3. ☐ An existing corporation changing to the tax year entered in item I, Part I.

P   Complete item P if the corporation is using the automatic approval provisions of Rev. Proc. 2002-38, 2002-22 I.R.B. 1037, to re quest (1) a natural business year (as defined in section 5.05 of Rev. Proc. 2002-38) or (2) a year that satisfies the ownership tax year test (as defined in section 5.06 of Rev. Proc. 2002-38). Check the applicable box below to indicate the representation statement the corporation is   making.

   1. Natural Business Year ▶ ☐ I represent that the corporation is adopting, retaining, or changing to a tax year that qualifies as its natural business year as defined in section 5.05 of Rev. Proc. 2002-38 and has attached a statement verifying that it satisfies the 25% gross receipts test (see instructions for content of statement). I also represent that the corporation is not precluded by section 4. 02 of Rev. Proc. 2002-38 from obtaining automatic approval of such adoption, retention, or change in tax year.

   2. Ownership Tax Year ▶ ☐ I represent that shareholders (as described in section 5.06 of Rev. Proc. 2002-38) holding more than half of the shares of the stock (as of the first day of the tax year to which the request relates) of the corporation have the same tax year or are concurrently changing to the tax year that the corporation adopts, retains, or changes to per item I, Part I, and that such year satisfies the requirement of section 4.01(3) of Rev. Proc. 2002-38. I also represent that the corporation is not precluded by section 4.0 2 of Rev. Proc. 2002-38 from obtaining automatic approval of such adoption, retention, or change in tax year.

Note: If you do not use item P and the corporation wants a fiscal tax year, complete either item Q or R below. Item Q is used to req uest a fiscal tax year based on a business purpose and to make a back-up section 444 election. Item R is used to make a regular section 444 election.

Q   Business Purpose— To request a fiscal tax year based on a business purpose, you must check box Q1. See instructions for details including payment of a user fee. You may also check box Q2 and/or box Q3.

   1. Check here ▶ ☐ if the fiscal year entered in item I, Part I, is requested under the prior approval provisions of Rev. Proc. 2002-39, 2002-22 I.R.B. 1046. Attach to Form 2553 a statement describing the relevant facts and circumstances and, if applicable, the gr oss receipts from sales and services necessary to establish a business purpose. See the instructions for details regarding the gross receipt s from sales and services. If the IRS proposes to disapprove the requested fiscal year, do you want a conference with the IRS National Offic e?
   ☐ Yes   ☐ No

   2. Check here ▶ ☐ to show that the corporation intends to make a back-up section 444 election in the event the corporation   s business purpose request is not approved by the IRS. (See instructions for more information.)

   3. Check here ▶ ☐ to show that the corporation agrees to adopt or change to a tax year ending December 31 if necessary for the IRS to accept this election for S corporation status in the event (1) the corporation s business purpose request is not approved and the corporation makes a back-up section 444 election, but is ultimately not qualified to make a section 444 election, or (2) the co rporation s business purpose request is not approved and the corporation did not make a back-up section 444 election.

R   Section 444 Election— To make a section 444 election, you must check box R1 and you may also check box R2.

   1. Check here ▶ ☐ to show the corporation will make, if qualified, a section 444 election to have the fiscal tax year shown in item I, Part I. To make the election, you must complete Form 8716, Election To Have a Tax Year Other Than a Required Tax Year, and either attach it to Form 2553 or file it separately.

   2. Check here ▶ ☐ to show that the corporation agrees to adopt or change to a tax year ending December 31 if necessary for the IRS to accept this election for S corporation status in the event the corporation is ultimately not qualified to make a section 444   election.

Part III Qualified Subchapter S Trust (QSST) Election Under Section 1361(d)(2)*

Income beneficiary s name and address	Social security number
Trust s name and address	Employer identification number

Date on which stock of the corporation was transferred to the trust (month, day, year)   . . . . ▶   /   /

In order for the trust named above to be a QSST and thus a qualifying shareholder of the S corporation for which this Form 2553 is filed, I hereby make the election under section 1361(d)(2). Under penalties of perjury, I certify that the trust meets the definitional requirements of section 1361(d)(3) and that all other information provided in Part III is true, correct, and complete.

_____   _____
Signature of income beneficiary or signature and title of legal representative or other qualified person making the election   Date

*Use Part III to make the QSST election only if stock of the corporation has been transferred to the trust on or before the dat e on which the corporation makes its election to be an S corporation. The QSST election must be made and filed separately if stock of the corp oration is transferred to the trust after the date on which the corporation makes the S election.

✪   Form 2553 (Rev. 12-2002)

Figure 4-1. Form 2553, Election by a Small Business Corporation (continued)

5

Tax Write-Offs and Special Deductions for Small Business

I F YOU WERE TO ASK YOUR ACCOUNTANT OR TAX ADVISOR WHAT A FRINGE BENEFIT is under the tax laws today, you might detect some uncertainty in his or her response. The term "fringe benefit" is not actually defined in the Internal Revenue Code. It is only by examples in the regulations that we are able to ascertain exactly what a fringe benefit is and how it can lower your tax bill.

As the owner of a small business, you are probably not interested in technical definitions or in any of the convoluted language that makes up the tax law today. Your only interest is to find out how you can claim every business deduction so you can survive in this high-tax atmosphere. This chapter will help you see how this works and help you better understand what it takes to get a legitimate tax write-off for your small business under the current law. Chapter 6 will address a special type of fringe benefit that makes for an additional tax advantage under the current law.

How to Make a Business Expense Deductible

To determine what kind of business expenses are allowed as deductions under the tax law, be aware of a catch-all section of the tax code that specifically states that any expense that is considered *ordinary and necessary* in the operation of your trade or business will qualify as a business deduction. Because this sounds so simple, some business owners accept the key phrase, *ordinary and necessary*, in the tax code as tacit approval to write off anything, as long as it has some connection with the business. After all, who is to argue over their interpretation of what is ordinary and necessary?

However, whether an expense is "ordinary and necessary" depends upon the facts surrounding each particular expense.

- First, an expense may be considered *ordinary* if it is the type that would normally be expected in the situation at hand even if the situation seldom arises.

- Second, an expense can be considered *necessary* if it is appropriate and helpful to your particular business or if it is clearly and reasonably related to your business.

If you have incurred a questionable business expense that you feel has met these tests, hold firm to your position. Don't let your accountant or even an IRS agent, for that matter, tell you otherwise. Remember, the tax code and the courts are on your side.

It is important to keep these reference standards handy when questionable expenses arise in the course of your business.

Typical Expenses Readily Accepted by the IRS

Some may argue that this rule authorizing you to write off anything ordinary and necessary is one of the most significant sections of the entire tax code. It provides for an infinite number of tax deductions for anyone who engages in any kind of trade or business. Further, when dealing with the common, everyday expenses of business, there is usually no problem in meeting the ordinary and necessary tests for the small business owner-operator.

The IRS will rarely raise a red flag when you take a deduction for the typical expense items found on most tax returns.

Simple titles given to your business expense deductions make a difference. Stay with the traditional terms and buzzwords.

These typical expenses include the following classifications:

- Cost of goods sold
- Office supplies
- Employee salaries
- Business taxes
- Repairs and maintenance
- Legal and accounting
- Travel and entertainment
- Insurance
- Licenses and permits
- Professional dues and fees
- Depreciation

Classifiers in the IRS Service Centers will expect these deductions to show up on most business tax returns, and inquiries are not usually raised unless there is concern over the dollar amounts claimed.

Be Aware of the Red Flag Alerts

Every return filed in an IRS Service Center is statistically graded to determine its potential for error. This procedure is referred to as the Discriminant Function System (DIF). From this scoring system, a DIF score is generated. With this, the IRS computer program is able to calculate the potential for error based on past audit experience. The DIF score identifies those returns that are more likely to contain errors and need an audit. What exactly makes up DIF scores is a very guarded secret of the IRS. However, be aware of two common items that can raise your DIF score and your chances of an audit.

RED FLAG #1

Deduction amounts that are higher than prescribed norms will send up a red flag to the IRS. Say, for example, you were to write off $18,000 in entertainment expenses for your small retail business that grosses only $100,000 per year. Chances are your DIF score would increase the odds of an audit even though those expenses may be thoroughly appropriate.

Red Flag #2

Unusual deductions, or those that are outside the typical expense categories will also result in a red flag. These deductions might include items like casualty losses or, perhaps, travel to the Caribbean to attend a planning seminar.

IRS audits have been becoming increasingly friendly, brief and to the point. However, be wary of the special temp program—and the "audit from hell."

As a small business owner, you need to be aware and track expenses incurred outside the everyday expense categories. Even if you are challenged, you will have the edge if you can demonstrate that the expense was an ordinary and necessary cost of carrying on your business endeavor.

News Alert: IRS Audit Message

In June 2002, the IRS commissioner announced to *The Wall Street Journal* that the IRS was resurrecting a special type of random audit—about 50,000 in 2002 alone. This news will cause many to think twice about throwing out those shoebox invoices and receipts that are stashed away in the basement.

The reason for the concern is that the audits are expected to be the so-called Taxpayer Compliance Measurement Program (TCMP), an audit program fraught with detailed interrogatories that could target every single item on your return. Dubbed "the audit from hell," the TCMP audit has been designed to give the IRS a real hard look at what taxpayers are writing off. This is also supposed to help the IRS refine its audit program and, to a large part, determine what red flags to use.

In general, the best advice is to take whatever deduction you are entitled to but make certain that you keep good records to back up whatever is claimed. Although the IRS has been auditing nearly a million returns overall in recent years, the majority of audits are usually an exercise with little trauma and relatively small cost to the taxpayer.

Fringe Benefits Help Answer the Red Flag Alert

In the IRS regulations, reference is made to a series of so-called fringe benefits. These are viewed as special tax write-offs that are automatical-

A side from the typical expenses that you can incur in business, another way to get an attractive write-off that will be accepted by the IRS classifiers is to provide a so-called fringe benefit to employees.

ly approved as ordinary and necessary costs of doing business. In short, unless they are unreasonable in amount, the IRS seldom raises a flag when they are spotted on your tax return. A partial summary of these fringe benefits includes the following:

- An employer-provided ticket to a sporting event or other entertainment
- Employer-provided discount on certain goods and services
- An employer-provided automobile
- A flight on an employer-provided aircraft
- Employer-provided discounts on commercial airline flights or free flights
- An employer-provided vacation

In one sense, the fringe benefits are a valuable tax advantage to the small business owner. In many instances they often provide a handsome tax write-off to a business just when it is most needed.

However, beware of an interesting twist in the law regarding these types of fringe benefits. Under normal circumstances, the assortment of fringe benefits, similar to the ones listed above, will probably be included in the income of the employee who receives the fringe benefit.

Further, if you are the owner of a corporation, as well as a working employee, and you have received the fringe benefit, you will end up paying personal income taxes on the fringe benefit windfall. The situation could get worse. You could be in the formidable 35 percent bracket under the most recent tax law if your combined fringe benefits and your personal income exceed $311,950 or $155,975 if married filing separately.

Q. What should I do before taking any fringe benefits from my corporation?
A. You should evaluate your own personal tax situation every time you take **any** kind of taxable benefit out of your business, whether it's a cash bonus or a certain fringe benefit. As shown in Chapter 1, your current tax bracket should help you decide if you want that benefit showing up on your tax return for that particular year.

One of the most common complaints of accountants and tax advisors is that small business clients all too often deviate from their planning regimen and pull out benefits from their corporations without considering their *personal* tax consequences. Whether it is a taxable fringe benefit or an ordinary salary bonus, they overlook that the day of reckoning is soon to appear—the often-dreaded April 15!

Many small business owner-operators are simply trying to be cost conscious during these economic times. Rationally, they simply can't afford to pay their advisors to do a professional analysis every time they need to take a few dollars out of the company.

How should you, as the owner-operator, handle your fringe benefits and special payments? It is increasingly imperative that you get a firm handle on your personal tax bracket for each operating year. This is especially important during these times of high tax rates and a tax code that seems to be continually revised.

Find out what federal tax bracket you are in and add Social Security and the state tax, if applicable. To do this, first you will need to make a current projection of your personal income for the year. Then, ask your accountant for a schedule of the individual tax rates set in the tax code at that particular time. (The rates for 2003 are included at the end of Chapter 1.)

If you are paying at the 35 percent marginal tax rate for that year and could arrange to keep your income down to a minimum for the following year, your action could help you push a bonus or a fringe benefit into a year with perhaps a 15 percent rate. This would amount to a personal tax savings of 20 percent.

Special Note: The following chapter discusses a special class of tax benefits that relieve the employee recipients from paying any tax whatever on the fringe benefit received.

Beware of Penalties and Interest for Failure to Pay

A secondary problem arises when, as a small corporation owner, your timing is bad when you are paying yourself fringe benefits and other special allowances. Penalties and interest may occur if taxes on those benefits are not paid on a timely basis.

Set your budget for estimated tax payments for your business earnings—if appropriate. Avoid unnecessary penalties and interest.

As personal tax rates rise, small business owners are taking a closer look at their personal tax bill. If they don't pay accordingly, the IRS computers will assess some tough interest penalties without failure.

Special Note: As a general rule, a penalty situation arises when 90 percent of the tax is not paid up front by withholding or estimating payments.

Below are some guidelines to avoid penalties and interest.

◆ Start paying estimated taxes at the end of the very next quarter following any of the special payments or fringe benefits you received from your business.

◆ Take a close look at the special exceptions that still apply to those who underestimate their tax liability. For example, even though there has been some tightening of the rules, many could avoid penalties by simply making estimated tax payments that match last year's tax bill. (See *Form 2210* at the end of this chapter to see which exceptions may apply to you.)

Remember, increasing your withholding at the very end of the year can spare you from penalty for not paying estimated taxes beforehand. In fact, many business owners treat this quirk in the law as a gaping loophole. To make the loophole work, however, you should apply a common-sense standard.

Some aggressive business owners have used this tactic to hold onto their entire withholding tax dollars for the entire year—interest free. The

Suppose you determine that you are going to be in a penalty situation because you will owe taxes on certain payments that you had received from the business earlier in the year. You should be aware that you cannot avoid the penalty by simply making an extra estimated payment in the last quarter. All payments must be made on time. Consider having your employer or corporation withhold additional amounts from your last paychecks during the remainder of the year. This will help you take advantage of a provision in the law that treats income tax withholding as if it had been paid equally throughout the entire year.

> **Illustration 5.1**
>
> Mort draws $60,000 in taxable fringe benefits at different intervals during the year from his wholly owned corporation.
>
> Although there was no tax paid in advance, Mort reasons that he could beat the system by simply waiting until December 31, and taking a paycheck with a big enough withholding amount to cover his federal tax bill for the entire year.
>
> For Mort, this seems like the perfect interest-free loan.

only reason it has worked is that the IRS has insufficient enforcement capability and human resources available to monitor this activity. There is word, however, that this activity will be looked at in the future, and some believe the chronic abusers will be subject to a host of other penalties for their action. For example, a false *W-4* form filing might become the subject of debate.

> P roceed to take advantage of the provision that allows you to treat withholding as if it had been paid equally throughout the entire year. But use this loophole for what it was apparently designed. In simple terms, take care of unpaid taxes on occasional income items for which there is no withholding. Most importantly, don't apply the procedure if the dollar amount of the late withholding payment appears to be excessive or beyond that which is reasonable.

Deductions for Special Payments to Shareholders to Eliminate Double Taxation

For many owners of small business corporations, there is one other situation that deserves special attention. This is the costly, potential double tax.

For many years, the IRS has made a special effort to charge a double tax to ordinary corporations that happen to provide special benefits to their owner-shareholders. Those supposedly privileged benefits were commonly labeled as "dividends" to the shareholders because, it was argued, they do not meet the definition of ordinary and necessary business expenses. Dividends, of course, are not usually deductible by a regular corporation and, hence, a double-tax usually prevails.

Tax planners tend to look closely at *any* special payment (such as year-end bonuses or periodic perks) that might flow to the owner-shareholder. There is always the fear that some IRS agent will contend that those unique gratuities were *not* payment for the services performed by the owner—even though that owner happens to be a regular employee.

Accordingly, wise owners of small corporations have become accustomed to taking a few simple steps to prevent the IRS from trying to second-guess the true value of their long hours and hard work. Salary authorization in the minutes accompanied by written documentation detailing the nature of the services performed is the best step to take to ensure their reasonableness and deductibility.

And Now, New Relief from the Double Tax

Thanks to a new tax law starting in 2003, most small owners of regular corporations will be spared from the full impact of the double tax. Under the new rules, many now feel that it makes little difference whether they take out money from the corporation in the form of a salary or a simple dividend. The reason? Under the new rules, dividends received from domestic corporations have been, for the most part, drastically reduced. In an effort to stimulate investment, Congress has reduced the tax on dividend to the same level as the newly lowered capital gains tax.

 Starting in 2003, the tax on dividends received was slashed to 15 percent—and even as low as 5 percent—for those in the lowest bracket.

Many view this generous tax cut as a windfall that Congress bestowed on investors in major corporations, i.e., the stock market. However, as the dust settles under the new rules, a host of planning opportunities for the small business owner has started to emerge. Most important, owners of small, regular corporations are beginning to find that pulling money out of their business as dividends might not be such a bad idea after all. With bare bones tax rates (possibly as low as 5 percent), who can complain? Further, who will care if some IRS agent decides, later on, that those special bonuses were nothing more than a disguised dividend paid to the small business owner?

Jones Corp., an ordinary corporation fully owned by May Jones, is ready to close the year with a $50,000 profit. Mary, who has no other

Don't be overly complacent with the new law provisions. It is true that, for the most part, the new tax rate on dividends is clearly a major tax advantage for most small business corporations. However, you still need to consider all the issues for the best tax planning results.

income, has not yet drawn anything for herself from the corporation and, because she needs all the cash possible, she inquires as to the best approach under the new law.

If Mary were to draw the full $50,000 as dividends from the corporation, the overall tax cost would be:

- Tax cost to Jones Corp. ($50,000 x 15 percent) $7,500

- Tax cost to Mary ($50,000 less $7,500 = $42,500 x 15 percent) $6,375

- Total tax liability $13,875

At first glance, it may seem that the dividend approach is the way to go. After all, who can argue with a 15 percent tax rate? However, the following considerations need to be examined to make an accurate calculation of projected tax cost:

- **The realistic tax cost to the corporation.** Remember, even though the corporation is paying at the lowest (15 percent) tax bracket, it is still paying some tax that, some would argue, *is wholly unnecessary*. This is why the corporation only has $42,500 remaining to pay Mary in our example.

- **The deductibility of salaries.** Unlike dividends, properly authorized salaries are fully deductible. If the corporation would pay Mary a $50,000 salary, there would be no corporate tax at all.

- **Mary's personal tax bracket.** Although Mary would only have had to pay a 15 percent tax on dividends, her tax cost on a one-time salary payment could vary greatly—depending on her personal deductions, credits, etc.

In short, it is possible that the decision to make a full $50,000 dividend declaration to Mary could be unproductive. Although unlikely, Mary *might* wind up paying *less* tax overall by taking out the $50,000 as a salary rather than as a dividend.

In addition, three important caveats need to be kept in mind every time you as a small corporation owner try to decide if you would be better off declaring dividends or paying a salary bonus.

1. The "reasonableness test" must be met with regard to any salaries paid to owner-shareholders. The IRS can readily take issue any time it appears that salaries paid to owners are out of line. In other words, you could just as easily be at risk by paying yourself an unreasonably *low* salary just to satisfy your tax objectives.

2. Don't forget the Social Security tax if you decide to pay additional salaries. With Social Security taxes as high as 15.6 percent (employer and employee combined) and other related costs, one needs to look closely at the real cost of adding salary costs to the corporation.

3. Carefully consider the value of additional retirement coverage with Social Security. All too often, struggling small business owners are hasty to eliminate the cost of Social Security for themselves. Although this cost is clearly a burden for many, be reminded that its potential benefits could be significant upon retirement. It pays to look ahead and measure these benefits within your own retirement plan.

Illustration 5.2

Delco, Inc., a small regular corporation, projected an $80,000 profit at year's end.

Delco's owner, Hortense, decided to take advantage of the new law and draw out the entire profit as a dividend rather than pay herself any salary for the year.

Later, calculations showed that Hortense had saved $333 overall by electing the dividend approach.

However, in addition to other possible risks, for a saving of $333, Hortense cut herself out of additional Social Security benefits upon retirement. The FICA tax on $80,000 (just under the maximum base) was never paid. Instead, Hortense paid a tax on the dividends received, which will allow her no credit at retirement.

The Reasonableness Test

It was shown earlier that all compensation paid for personal services must be reasonable to be deductible. When the payee is a shareholder, close scrutiny is sure to follow. What is reasonable is specific to the situation and, thus, hard-and-fast rules don't exist. There are, however, guidelines set for the IRS by the courts, which give some clues as to what the IRS will look for. There are five suggested factors for determining whether compensation paid to a shareholder is reasonable.

1. The role that the shareholder plays in the company
2. Salaries paid by similar companies for comparable services
3. The character and financial condition of the company
4. Any conflicts between the employees' personal and business interest relative to the corporation's, which might make it easier for nondeductible dividends to be disguised as salaries or deductible fringe benefits
5. Internal consistency (attention is directed to the past history of the corporation's compensation pattern and whether or not it was reasonably and consistently followed)

Chapter Summary

All business expenses must meet certain guidelines before they will be deemed deductible under the current law. In general, they must be considered ordinary and necessary in the operation of your business. Certain commonly used expenses (including many fringe benefits) are expected to be found in small business, and normally, do not raise the DIF score and chances for audit scrutiny.

Also, regular corporations must be careful. To gain a full tax deduction for any salary or benefit to owner-shareholders, certain guidelines must be followed.

Form 4868

Department of the Treasury
Internal Revenue Service (99)

Application for Automatic Extension of Time To File U.S. Individual Income Tax Return

OMB No. 1545-0188

2002

It's Convenient, Safe, and Secure

IRS *e file* is the IRS's electronic filing program. Now you can get an automatic extension of time to file your tax return by filing Form 4868 electronically. You will receive an electronic acknowledgment or confirmation number once you complete the transaction. Keep it with your records. **Do not** send in Form 4868 if you file electronically.

Complete Form 4868 to use as a worksheet. If you think you may owe tax when you file your return, you will need to estimate your total tax liability and subtract how much you have already paid (lines 4, 5, and 6 below).

If you think you may owe tax and wish to make a payment, you may pay by electronic funds withdrawal using option 1 or 2 below or you may pay by credit card using option 3.

1 ☎ E-file by Phone—February 13–April 15
Call toll free **1-888-796-1074**

Anyone who filed a tax return for 2001 or 2000 can file Form 4868 by phone. The telephone system will accept extensions any time from February 13 through April 15, 2003, and your extension will be good through August 15, 2003. Filing by telephone is advantageous because it is free and you get a confirmation number.

If you wish to make a payment by electronic funds withdrawal you will be asked for the adjusted gross income (AGI) from your 2001 or 2000 tax return. Your AGI for these years is located on line 33 of your Form 1040, line 19 of your 1040A, line 4 of your 1040EZ, or line 1 of your Tele-file Tax Record. If you choose, you may also file your extension by phone and mail a payment to the address shown in the middle column on page 4.

2 🖥 E-file Using Your Personal Computer or Through a Tax Professional

Refer to your tax software package or tax preparer for ways to file electronically. Be sure to have a copy of last year's tax return

— you will be asked to provide information from the return for taxpayer verification. If you wish to make a payment, you can pay by electronic funds withdrawal (see page 4) or send your payment to the address shown in the middle column on page 4.

3 💳 E-file and Pay by Credit Card

You can get an extension if you pay part or all of your estimate of income tax due by using a credit card (American Express Card, Discover Card, MasterCard card, or Visa card). Your payment must be at least $1. You may pay by phone or over the Internet through one of the service providers listed below.

Each service provider will charge a convenience fee based on the amount of the tax payment you are making. Fees may vary between service providers. You will be told what the fee is during the transaction and will have the option to continue or cancel the transaction. You may also obtain the convenience fee by calling the service providers' automated customer service numbers or visiting their web sites. All calls are toll free. Do not add the convenience fee to your tax payment.

Official Payments Corporation	Link2Gov Corporation
1-800-2PAY-TAX	1-888-PAY-1040
(1-800-272-9829)	(1-888-729-1040)
1-877-754-4413 (Customer Service)	1-888-658-5465 (Customer Service)
www.officialpayments.com	www.PAY1040.com

Form 709 or 709-A. Although an extension of time to file your income tax return also extends the time to file Form 709 or 709-A, you cannot make payments of the gift or GST tax with a credit card. To make a payment of the gift or GST tax, send a check or money order to the service center where the donor's income tax return will be filed. Enter "2002 Form 709" and the donor's name and social security number on the payment.

🖊 File a Paper Form 4868

If you wish to file on paper instead of electronically, fill in the Form 4868 below and mail it to the address shown on page 4.

▼ DETACH HERE ▼

Form 4868

Department of the Treasury
Internal Revenue Service (99)

Application for Automatic Extension of Time To File U.S. Individual Income Tax Return

For calendar year 2002, or other tax year beginning , 2002, ending ,

OMB No. 1545-0188

2002

Part I Identification		**Part III** Individual Income Tax	
1 Your name(s) (see instructions)		**4** Estimate of total tax liability for 2002 $	
Address (see instructions)		**5** Total 2002 payments	
City, town or post office, state, and ZIP code		**6 Balance due.** Subtract 5 from 4 . .	
2 Your social security number	**3** Spouse's social security number	**Part IV** Gift/GST Tax—If you are **not filing** a gift or GST tax return, go to Part V now. See the instructions.	
		7 Your gift or GST tax payment . $	
		8 Your spouse's gift/GST tax payment	

Part II Complete ONLY If Filing Gift/GST Tax Return

Part V Total

Caution: Only for gift/GST tax extension! Checking box(es) may result in correspondence if Form 709 or 709-A is not filed.

9 Total liability. Add lines 6, 7, and 8 $

This form also extends the time for filing a gift or generation skipping transfer (GST) tax return if you file a calendar (not fiscal) year income tax return. Enter your gift or GST tax payment(s) in Part IV and:

10 Amount you are paying . . . . ▶

Confirmation Number

Check this box ▶ ☐ if you are requesting a **Gift or GST tax return** extension.

Check this box ▶ ☐ if your spouse is requesting a **Gift or GST tax return** extension.

If you file electronically, you will receive a confirmation number telling you that your Form 4868 has been accepted. Enter the confirmation number here and keep it for your records . . . . ▶

For Privacy Act and Paperwork Reduction Act Notice, see page 4.

Cat. No. 13141W

Form **4868** (2002)

Form 4868

Form **2210**	Underpayment of	OMB No. 1545-0140
Department of the Treasury Internal Revenue Service	Estimated Tax by Individuals, Estates, and Trusts ▶ See separate instructions. ▶ Attach to Form 1040, 1040A, 1040NR, 1040NR-EZ, or 1041.	**2002** Attachment Sequence No. 06

Name(s) shown on tax return	Identifying number

In most cases, you do not need to file Form 2210. The IRS will figure any penalty you owe and send you a bill. File Form 2210 only if one or more boxes in Part I apply to you. If you do not need to file Form 2210, you still may use it to figure your penalty. Enter the amount from Part III, line 22, or Part IV, line 36, on the penalty line of your return, but do not attach Form 2210.

Part I Reasons for Filing— If 1a, 1b, or 1c below applies to you, you may be able to lower or eliminate your penalty. But you **must** check the boxes that apply and file Form 2210 with your tax return. If 1d below applies to you, check that box and file Form 2210 with your tax return.

1   Check whichever boxes apply (if none apply, see the text above Part I and do not file Form 2210):

a ☐ You request a waiver. In certain circumstances, the IRS will waive all or part of the penalty. See Waiver of Penalty on page 1 of the instructions.

b ☐ You use the annualized income installment method.   If your income varied during the year, this method may reduce the amount of one or more required installments. See page 4 of the instructions.

c ☐ You had Federal income tax withheld from wages and, for estimated tax purposes, you treat the withheld tax as paid on the dates it was actually withheld, instead of in equal amounts on the payment due dates. See the instructions for line 23 on page 2.

d ☐ Your required annual payment (line 15 below) is based on your 2001 tax and you filed or are filing a joint return for either 2001 or 2002 but not for both years.

Part II   Required Annual Payment

2	Enter your 2002 tax after credits (see page 2 of the instructions)	2
3	Other taxes (see page 2 of the instructions)	3
4	Add lines 2 and 3	4
5	Earned income credit ... 5	
6	Additional child tax credit ... 6	
7	Credit for Federal tax paid on fuels ... 7	
8	Health insurance credit for eligible recipients ... 8	
9	Add lines 5 through 8	9
10	Current year tax. Subtract line 9 from line 4	10
11	Multiply line 10 by 90% (.90) ... 11	
12	Withholding taxes. Do not include any estimated tax payments on this line (see page 2 of the instructions)	12
13	Subtract line 12 from line 10. If less than $1,000, stop here; you do not owe the penalty. Do not file Form 2210	13
14	Enter the tax shown on your 2001 tax return (112% of that amount if the adjusted gross income shown on that return is more than $150,000, or, if married filing separately for 2002, more than $75,000). Caution: See page 2 of the instructions	14
15	Required annual payment. Enter the smaller of line 11 or line 14	15

If line 12 is equal to or more than line 15, stop here; you do not owe the penalty.
Do not file Form 2210 unless you checked box 1d above.

Part III   Short Method (Caution: See page 2 of the instructions to find out if you can use the short method. If you checked box 1b or 1c in Part I, skip this part and go to Part IV.)

16	Enter the amount, if any, from line 12 above ... 16	
17	Enter the total amount, if any, of estimated tax payments you made 17	
18	Add lines 16 and 17	18
19	Total underpayment for year. Subtract line 18 from line 15. If zero or less, stop here; you do not owe the penalty. Do not file Form 2210 unless you checked box 1d above	19
20	Multiply line 19 by .03713	20
21	● If the amount on line 19 was paid on or after 4/15/03, enter -0-. ● If the amount on line 19 was paid before 4/15/03, make the following computation to find the amount to enter on line 21. Amount on line 19 × Number of days paid before 4/15/03 × .00014	21
22	Penalty. Subtract line 21 from line 20. Enter the result here and on Form 1040, line 74; Form 1040A, line 48; Form 1040NR, line 73; Form 1040NR-EZ, line 26; or Form 1041, line 26, but do not file Form 2210 unless you checked one or more of the boxes in Part I above . . ▶	22

For Paperwork Reduction Act Notice, see page 5 of separate instructions.	Cat. No. 11744P	Form **2210** (2002)

Form 2210 (continued on next two pages)

Part IV   Regular Method   (See page 2 of the instructions if you are filing Form 1040NR or 1040NR-EZ.)

Section A —Figure Your Underpayment		Payment Due Dates			
		(a) 4/15/02	(b) 6/15/02	(c) 9/15/02	(d) 1/15/03
23	Required installments. If box 1b applies, enter the amounts from Schedule AI, line 25. Otherwise, enter 25% (.25) of line 15, Form 2210, in each column				
24	Estimated tax paid and tax withheld (see page 2 of the instructions). For column (a) only, also enter the amount from line 24 on line 28. If line 24 is equal to or more than line 23 for all payment periods, stop here; you do not owe the penalty. Do not file Form 2210 unless you checked a box in Part I . . .				
	Complete lines 25 through 31 of one column before going to the next column.				
25	Enter amount, if any, from line 31 of previous column				
26	Add lines 24 and 25				
27	Add amounts on lines 29 and 30 of the previous column				
28	Subtract line 27 from line 26. If zero or less, enter -0-. For column (a) only, enter the amount from line 24 .				
29	If the amount on line 28 is zero, subtract line 26 from line 27. Otherwise, enter -0-				
30	Underpayment. If line 23 is equal to or more than line 28, subtract line 28 from line 23. Then go to line 25 of next column. Otherwise, go to line 31 . ▶				
31	Overpayment. If line 28 is more than line 23, subtract line 23 from line 28. Then go to line 25 of next column				

Section B —Figure the Penalty   (Complete lines 32 through 35 of one column before going to the next column.)

			4/15/02	6/15/02	9/15/02	
Rate Period 1		April 16, 2002 —December 31, 2002	Days:	Days:	Days:	
	32	Number of days from the date shown above line 32 to the date the amount on line 30 was paid or 12/31/02, whichever is earlier				
	33	Underpayment on line 30 (see page 3 of the instructions) × days on line 32 / 365 × .06 ▶	$	$	$	
		January 1, 2003 —April 15, 2003	12/31/02	12/31/02	12/31/02	1/15/03
Rate Period 2			Days:	Days:	Days:	Days:
	34	Number of days from the date shown above line 34 to the date the amount on line 30 was paid or 4/15/03, whichever is earlier				
	35	Underpayment on line 30 (see page 4 of the instructions) × days on line 34 / 365 × .05 ▶	$	$	$	$

36   Penalty. Add all amounts on lines 33 and 35 in all columns. Enter the total here and on Form 1040, line 74; Form 1040A, line 48; Form 1040NR, line 73; Form 1040NR-EZ, line 26; or Form 1041, line 26, but do not file Form 2210 unless you checked one or more of the boxes in Part I . ▶   36 $

Form 2210 (continued)

Tax Write-Offs and Special Deductions for Small Business

Form 2210 (2002)   Page 3

Schedule AI —Annualized Income Installment Method   (See pages 4 and 5 of the instructions.)

Estates and trusts, do not use the period ending dates shown to the right.
Instead, use the following: 2/28/02, 4/30/02, 7/31/02, and 11/30/02.

		(a) 1/1/02–3/31/02	(b) 1/1/02–5/31/02	(c) 1/1/02–8/31/02	(d) 1/1/02–12/31/02
Part I	**Annualized Income Installments**				
1	Enter your adjusted gross income for each period (see instructions). (Estates and trusts, enter your taxable income without your exemption for each period.) . . . . [1]				
2	Annualization amounts. (Estates and trusts, see instructions.) . . [2]	4	2.4	1.5	1
3	Annualized income. Multiply line 1 by line 2 . . . . [3]				
4	Enter your itemized deductions for the period shown in each column. If you do not itemize, enter -0- and skip to line 7. (Estates and trusts, enter -0-, skip to line 9, and enter the amount from line 3 on line 9.) [4]				
5	Annualization amounts . . . . [5]	4	2.4	1.5	1
6	Multiply line 4 by line 5 (see instructions if line 3 is more than $68,650) [6]				
7	In each column, enter the full amount of your standard deduction from Form 1040, line 38, or Form 1040A, line 24 (Form 1040NR or 1040NR-EZ filers, enter -0-. Exception: Indian students and business apprentices, enter standard deduction from Form 1040NR, line 36, or Form 1040NR-EZ, line 11.) . . . . [7]				
8	Enter the larger of line 6 or line 7. . . . . [8]				
9	Subtract line 8 from line 3 . . . . [9]				
10	In each column, multiply $3,000 by the total number of exemptions claimed (see instructions if line 3 is more than $103,000). (Estates and trusts and Form 1040NR or 1040NR-EZ filers, enter the exemption amount shown on your tax return.) . . . . . . [10]				
11	Subtract line 10 from line 9 . . . . [11]				
12	Figure your tax on the amount on line 11 (see instructions) . . . [12]				
13	Form 1040 filers only, complete Part II and enter your self-employment tax from line 34 below . . . . [13]				
14	Enter other taxes for each payment period (see instructions) . . [14]				
15	Total tax. Add lines 12, 13, and 14 . . . . [15]				
16	For each period, enter the same type of credits as allowed on Form 2210, lines 2 and 9 (see instructions) . . . . [16]				
17	Subtract line 16 from line 15. If zero or less, enter -0- . . . . [17]				
18	Applicable percentage . . . . [18]	22.5%	45%	67.5%	90%
19	Multiply line 17 by line 18 . . . . [19]				
	Caution: Complete lines 20–25 of one column before going to the next column.				
20	Add the amounts in all previous columns of line 25 . . . . . [20]	////			
21	Subtract line 20 from line 19. If zero or less, enter -0- . . . . [21]				
22	Enter 25% (.25) of line 15 on page 1 of Form 2210 in each column [22]				
23	Subtract line 25 of the previous column from line 24 of the previous column . . . . [23]	////			
24	Add lines 22 and 23 and enter the total . . . . [24]				
25	Enter the smaller of line 21 or line 24 here and on Form 2210, line 23 . . . . ▶ [25]				
Part II	**Annualized Self-Employment Tax**				
26	Net earnings from self-employment for the period (see instructions) [26]				
27	Prorated social security tax limit . . . . [27]	$21,225	$35,375	$56,600	$84,900
28	Enter actual wages for the period subject to social security tax or the 6.2% portion of the 7.65% railroad retirement (tier 1) tax . . [28]				
29	Subtract line 28 from line 27. If zero or less, enter -0- . . . . [29]				
30	Annualization amounts . . . . [30]	0.496	0.2976	0.186	0.124
31	Multiply line 30 by the smaller of line 26 or line 29 . . . . . [31]				
32	Annualization amounts . . . . [32]	0.116	0.0696	0.0435	0.029
33	Multiply line 26 by line 32 . . . . [33]				
34	Add lines 31 and 33. Enter the result here and on line 13 above ▶ [34]				

⊕   Form **2210** (2002)

Form 2210 (continued)

63

6

Tax-Sheltered Employer-Provided Fringe Benefits

As was pointed out in the previous chapter, certain fringe benefits make for nice tax deductions in a business operation. In fact, as long as they are reasonable in amount, the IRS seldom raises questions when they are deducted on a business tax return. The one downside, however, is that this class of fringe benefits usually ends up on the employee's tax return and is fully taxed at the ordinary rates.

The general rationale of the tax law is unless a fringe benefit is excluded from income by some special provision in the tax code, it must be included in the employee's income.

There is a class of fringe benefits specifically exempted from income because of certain language in the tax code. Chapter 3 shows how the special tax break applies to benefits like health and accident plans. This chapter will focus on other fringe benefits and provide you with guidelines on how to qualify for tax-sheltered treatment. If you are a small business owner, you will find these provisions particularly appealing. The benefits will not be denied to you just because you are the owner and employee.

Key Observation: It is important to note that these specifically defined fringe benefits get the maximum benefit when used by regular corporations.

If you own more than 2 percent of an S corporation or an LLC, the deduction will be allowed, but the fringe benefit must be reported as income.

On one hand, your business gets a full tax write-off for the fringe benefit made available. On the other hand, you, as the owner, may not have to pay one cent in taxes on the benefits paid. Take a look at the fringe benefits that are eligible for the tax-sheltered treatment.

Meals and Lodging Furnished by the Employer

An important tax-free windfall that extends to the employees of a business enterprise is that of meals and lodging that may be provided in the course of employment. Although this particular benefit only works with ordinary corporations when it involves owner-employees, all business operators should be aware of its existence.

With an ordinary corporation, employees can reap sizable tax savings if they receive meals and lodging on a continuing basis. What you need to do, however, is be able to show that the corporate employer gained some benefit in the process. In other words, you should be prepared to demonstrate that the employee isn't the only one getting value when this fringe benefit is made available.

What does the tax code say about meals? The value of meals furnished to the employee, his or her spouse, or dependents are tax free when

> It pays to know which business deductions are recognized as real fringe benefits.

- ◆ they are furnished for the employer's convenience and
- ◆ they are furnished on the employer's business premises.

WHAT "CONVENIENCE OF THE EMPLOYER" MEANS

"Convenience of the employer" implies that the employee's continued presence on the employer's premises is necessary to better perform duties properly or supervise others. Typically, this is the case when the employee is expected to handle emergency calls or special situations with short notice.

The meals are considered to be for the convenience of the employer if they are furnished for a "noncompensatory business reason" of the employer whether

> **B**e prepared to show that there were sound business reasons that do not include compensatory reasons for making the meals available. If it appears that the employer was merely trying to pass off some extra benefits or compensation to the employee, it won't work.

- ◆ they are free of charge or
- ◆ they are for a flat fee, whether or not the employee accepts the meals.

Meals given to promote goodwill, better morale, or merely to attract prospective employees will be considered compensatory and taxable.

WHAT THE TAX CODE SAYS ABOUT LODGING PROVIDED BY AN EMPLOYER

The rules for excludability are the same as for meals except that one additional tough requirement is added: the lodging must be accepted as a condition of employment.

Key Observation: It is important to note that meals and lodging made available to employees will not be disqualified for the special tax-free treatment just because those employees happen to be stockholder-owners.

Illustration 6.1

Excel Corporation provided lodging to Fred, one of its major stockholders. Fred is a corporate officer and manager of the company farm.

Because of the requirement that Fred be accessible at all times for the day-to-day management of the farm, the value of his lodging was excluded from his income.

Additionally, because meals were furnished on the business premises and were for the convenience of the employer, they too were excluded from Fred's income as well as from the income of other employees.

Dependent Care Assistance Programs

This tax break may be of interest to employees who have dependent children who are physically challenged or are under age 13 and require child care during their parents' absence. The dependent care assistance program can also benefit you as an owner or principal shareholder as long as certain qualifications are met. The amount of dependent care assistance you can provide with a direct tax credit is up to $5,000. If you are married filing separately, the maximum is $2,500. Dependent care assistance can include the following:

◆ The cost of baby sitters, day camp, nursery schools, or other outside-the-home costs

◆ Employment-related household expenses—including domestic services in your home, such as laundry, cleaning, and cooking

How Does It Work?

A certain portion of the payments made by the employer for dependent care can be excluded from income, whether they are paid to the caregiver directly or simply reimbursed to the employee. The special exclusion does not apply to employer-provided dependent care if payments are made to

◆ individuals for whom the employee is entitled to take a dependency exemption or

◆ children of the employee who are under age 13.

There are certain restrictions against discrimination in favor of shareholder-owners and highly compensated employees.

Key Observation: A self-employed individual is recognized for these purposes as an employee. By definition, any self-employed individual who can be covered under a self-employed retirement plan may participate in dependent assistance care programs. They too can receive dependent care assistance that is excludable from income.

Another distinct advantage that must not be overlooked is that the self-employed individual receiving the benefits could also deduct the cost of providing the benefit.

It is important to put it in writing. Make sure you spell out the details of the dependent care plan. Remember, the employees must be notified of the existence of the plan, the eligibility to participate, and all the relevant terms.

Exclusion for No-Additional Cost Services

This tax-sheltered fringe benefit applies to the value of services provided to employees and their dependents for a reduced charge or no charge at all. Generally, it is free from tax to the employee if it can be shown that the employer sells the same service to nonemployee customers in the ordinary course of business in which the employee works. The key to making this benefit work lies in being able to demonstrate that

♦ the employer incurs no substantial additional cost in providing such services to the employee, and

♦ the exclusion does not discriminate in favor of highly compensated employees.

One way to fit the definition of a no-additional-cost service is to understand the term *excess capacity services*. This refers to services that are available for use and would remain unused if the employees did not use them; the following are examples of this idea:

♦ Hotel accommodations

♦ Aircraft transportation

♦ Train, bus, or cruise line transportation

Q. What does the phrase "the employer must have incurred no substantial additional costs" for the services rendered really mean?
A. The determination of substantial additional costs is handled on a case-by-case basis. Generally, it involves the cost of labor, materials, supplies, and other nonlabor costs.

♦ Telephone services

When trying to determine if the employer has incurred a substantial additional cost, you should not confuse the definition with the fact that the employee might have reimbursed the employer for the cost of providing the service. Accordingly, any reimbursements made for the cost of the service has nothing to do with the question involving whether or not the employer has incurred a substantial additional cost.

Illustration 6.2
Roadway Corporation is in the business of repairing computers and various types of electronic equipment. Roadway notified its employees that it would repair its employees' personal computer equipment at no charge.

> During the year, Roadway repairs Sue's personal computer but in the process incurs the substantial additional cost of $150 for materials. The total value of the repair service was $600.
>
> Sue offers to pay the additional cost of $150 with the expectation that this would make her eligible to exclude the entire benefit from income.
>
> Unfortunately, the amount of the $450 benefit ($600 minus $150) is fully taxable. It makes no difference if Sue reimburses Roadway for that portion of the cost. The fact is, a substantial additional cost was still incurred.
>
> However, if the additional cost incurred were for some minor supplies in the amount of $35, the value of the benefit would more than likely be fully excludable.

Exclusion for Qualified Employee Discounts

Discounts on qualified property or services that are taken by employees, their spouses, and children can turn into an attractive tax-free benefit in certain circumstances. The benefit refers to the right to exclude from income the discount savings as long as

- ◆ the amount of the discount does not exceed certain limitations and
- ◆ there is not discrimination among the higher-paid employees.

What is the definition of *qualified property or services?* The term refers to property and services that are normally offered for sale to outside customers in the ordinary course of business. Certain specific property, however, is not eligible by definition, including real property (residential real estate) and personal property commonly held for investment. In other words, this includes any kind of tangible or nontangible property commonly held for investment.

> **Illustration 6.3**
>
> Chester is a consultant with a small stock brokerage firm that gives him a discount for commissions on security transactions and on stocks and bonds that he buys directly from the firm for his own account.
>
> Chester can exclude the discount on the commissions from his income, which is also subject to the limitations for discounts on services.
>
> Chester cannot exclude the discount on the purchase of securities for his own account since the securities do not meet the definition of qualified property.

Key Observation: Determine the limitations on the tax-free exclusions for property and services. The amount that can be excluded from income as a qualified employee discount on property sold to the employee is limited to the **gross profit percentage.** This means the gross profit percentage of the price that the merchandise would have been offered to outside customers is tax free. Of course, if the employee discount is in excess of this amount, that excess must be included in the employee's gross income and taxed accordingly.

Exclusion for Working Condition Fringe Benefits

There are instances when certain items of property or services are provided to an employee and will not be charged to that employee's income. General conditions that need to be met for this tax-sheltered provision include the following:

- First, the cost of property or services would have ordinarily been deductible by the employee, had the employee paid for them.
- Second, the deduction would have been allowable as an ordinary and necessary business deduction for the employee in connection with the trade or business.

This may be easier to understand by just observing some examples of the business expense items that fit in this category. These include the following:

- Employer-paid subscriptions for business journals and periodicals
- Use of employer-provided vehicles for business purposes
- Employer payment for on-the-job training
- Employer-paid business travel for employees
- Educational assistance programs

The requirement that the expense would have to be deductible as an expense in connection with that trade or business is important to understand. For example, consider the fringe benefit arrangement discussed in Illustration 6.4.

> **Illustration 6.4**
>
> Donald allows for physical examinations under a special program for his employees, Maria and Harold.
>
> The cost of the examinations **is not tax free** and must be included in both Maria's and Harold's income.
>
> Even though the cost of medical examinations would ordinarily be deductible as a medical expense, such costs would not have been deductible as an ordinary and necessary business expense of the employees involved.
>
> Had Donald provided for payment of the employees' professional dues or subscriptions to business journals, the employees would have been able to exclude the same as a working condition fringe benefit.

The nondiscrimination rules do not apply except in unusual circumstances, such as with product testing programs. For example, if you provide personal computers for the business use of certain officers and managers in the company, the officers and managers can exclude the cost from their income even though the other employees are not entitled to this fringe benefit.

 Working condition fringe benefits can make for substantial tax savings.

Employer-Provided Transportation

You will recall that one of the ground rules for a working condition fringe to be nontaxable to the employee is that the expense must pass a deductibility test. More specifically, the expense must be ordinarily deductible had it been incurred by that employee in the course of that employee's trade or business. In spite of all the changes in the tax law in recent years, travel expenses and automobile expenses are still deductible when incurred in business.

The definition of employer-provided transportation is all-inclusive; thus tax-free treatment as a working condition fringe can extend to items such as

- automobiles made available to employees,
- air flights,
- chauffeur services,
- taxis, and

♦ miscellaneous local transportation.

Note that the employee can receive these benefits tax free only when used on employer business. Commuting and personal use render the value of the services taxable.

Q. How do the working condition fringe benefit rules apply to an ordinary automobile that is made available for an employee's use?

A. It is clear from reading the tax rules that the use of an automobile qualifies for tax-free treatment under the working condition fringe rules. This is because automobile expense is one of the most typical trade or business expenses that an employee can incur.

Illustration 6.5

Bold Company purchases a new automobile, which it makes available to its major shareholder, Herb.

Herb uses the car solely for business, as he needs to travel along a particular sales route.

The value of the car is totally tax free to Herb since he would ordinarily have been allowed to deduct the cost of an automobile in his particular work.

Suppose Bold Company actually provides two cars to Herb, but one is used solely by his wife, who does not participate in the business. In that case, Herb will be taxed only on the value of the second car.

In real-life circumstances, a situation like Herb's, involving 100 percent business use of an automobile, is somewhat far fetched.

It is only in the most unique circumstances that a working employee could demonstrate that the automobile is solely driven for business.

Key Observation: IRS auditors may have become a bit more tolerant of the tough record-keeping rules imposed on the operators of business autos. In almost all cases, however, they still make some analyses during an audit, separating business from personal mileage. Unless you have a meticulous log of your business miles, kept on a contemporaneous basis, it is likely that you will incur an adjustment resulting in additional tax liability.

As an employer, you may be able to eliminate this burdensome record-keeping requirement. If you have a written policy that generally prohibits personal employees from using a car for personal use or if you include the full annual value of the car in an employee's wages, then you will not have to keep the meticulous log of business miles.

Special Note: The toughest cases are the ones involving commuting expenses that are never deductible as a business expense. In almost all cases, there is some element of commuting for an employee who leaves his or her home to begin a workday. A notable exception is when the small business owner has a bona-fide home office.

VEHICLES USED PARTIALLY FOR NONBUSINESS PURPOSES

If you, like most employees, use your employer-provided automobile for personal use from time to time, you need to refer to a simple formula to determine the tax consequences. Here is the formula:

The value of the vehicle's availability (per IRS tables)
Multiplied by the ratio* between business and personal miles
(*ratio = business miles divided by total miles)
Equals the working condition fringe benefit (tax free)

Illustration 6.6

Sharp Company provides a car for its employee, Rose.

The value of the car for the year is $3,000 to Rose if she were to use it 100 percent of the time.

During the year, Rose drives the car 7,000 business miles for the company and 3,000 personal miles. 10,000 total miles were driven during the year.

By applying the formula, the tax-free working condition fringe is calculated.
$3,000 (the value of the vehicle's availability)
Multiplied by .70 or 70 percent (the ratio of business car use)
Equals $2,100 (the working condition fringe benefit)

See Chapter 10 for more information on the use of business automobiles.

In the event the employer is a corporation of which the employee is a major shareholder, take caution when cars are provided with little or no business purpose. The extra compensation might be viewed as a dividend to the shareholder if the overall compensation is deemed to be unreasonable. Don't forget the tough, double tax problems associat-

Even if you happen to generate a tax liability because of the personal use of a company-provided vehicle, you should be aware that the cost would still be less than if you leased the car. It would also, more than likely, be cheaper than if you bought and financed the car on your own.

ed with dividends to corporation shareholders.

Employer-Paid Trips

Many employees, including officers of companies, often receive expense-paid trips that combine elements of business with pleasure. To determine whether or not the cost of these trips is a taxable event to the employee, you need to evaluate the primary purpose for taking the trip.

Determine if an employer-paid trip is primarily business in nature. In reviewing the relevant facts for determining the business or personal nature of employer-paid trips, you begin to readily appreciate the value of keeping written records in business. Some of the factors that are brought into the equation are

- the amount of actual time spent on business, as opposed to pleasure;
- the geographic considerations; and
- the general attitude and position of the employer.

For example, if a business meeting is held at a luxury resort, a non-business tone already exists. If that employer looks to the occasion as primarily a pleasurable event while passing out written memos regarding this issue, then a nonbusiness purpose probably will be inferred. Remember, no factor is conclusive by itself. Training and professional development for the business is a strong indication that a trip is primarily business-related.

THE KEY TEST

No income will result to the employee if, from the employee's point of view,

- the trip was primarily business in nature and
- the employee did not spend a significant amount of time pursuing personal benefit and enjoyment.

If you can demonstrate that the primary purpose of the trip was personal, then the value of the trip will be taxable income. Each case is judged by its own facts and circumstances.

Illustration 6.7

ARC Employees Monte and Oscar went to Miami to observe a new software program related to their business operations.

The trip lasted four days, and a major portion of their time was devoted to sharing technical ideas at business sessions and dinner meetings.

Even though ARC emphasized a holiday-like tone when it tried to stimulate employee participation, the trip will probably be deemed primarily business and tax free to Monte and Oscar.

Illustration 6.8

Later that year, ARC paid for its business manager, Victoria, a 33-percent shareholder, to go to London to learn about a manufacturing process ARC planned to introduce.

During Victoria's stay, she met with several business owners and potential suppliers but failed to keep records of such.

After she returned, neither she nor ARC could produce minutes of business meetings, business reports, or even a corporate resolution authorizing her to go on the fact-finding mission.

This lack of documentation required Victoria to report the entire trip as income.

Employer-Provided Parking

If you provide your employees with free parking, you might just find that they can exclude that allowance from their income. As long as you meet the definition of *qualified parking*, the payments for such can be treated as a nontaxable transportation fringe.

Special Note: Since 1998, new restrictions disqualify this benefit if it is provided "in lieu of taxable compensation."

WHAT IS QUALIFIED PARKING?

Qualified parking refers to parking that is provided to an employee. Qualified parking does not include parking at a facility located on or near the employee's personal residence, which means a self-employed individual cannot qualify under this definition if she or he works from home. It also means that the actual parking facility must be located either on or near the employer's business premises or at or near a location from which the employee commutes to work by mass transit or hired commuter vehicle.

Illustration 6.9

Road Corporation provides a parking allowance for its managing officers, Ed and Jill.

Ed parks his car in a lot located directly across the street from the office.

Jill's parking location is in an old lot next to a train station located two blocks from her home.

Ed can treat his parking fringe as a tax-free benefit; however, Jill will be taxed on the allowance, because the facility is near her personal residence.

It is important to remember that Road does not have to satisfy any nondiscrimination rules to qualify parking for the tax-free treatment as a working condition fringe benefit.

Employer-Provided Commuter Transportation

Transportation that is provided to an employee for commuting may, in certain cases, be considered a nontaxable transportation fringe. To qualify for this tax-free benefit, the transportation must be provided in a *commuter highway vehicle,* and it must involve transportation between the employee's residence and the place of employment only.

WHAT IS A COMMUTER HIGHWAY VEHICLE?

A commuter highway vehicle is any highway vehicle that has the following characteristics:

- ◆ A seating capacity of at least six adults, not including the driver
- ◆ Eighty percent of its mileage is incurred in transporting employees between their residences and the place of employment.
- ◆ Eighty percent of its mileage can reasonably be expected to be on commuting trips in which the vehicle is filled to at least one-half capacity by employees.

For example, if your company uses a highway vehicle with a seating capacity of eight, not including the driver, it must be reasonably expected that 80 percent of the total mileage of the vehicle, for a particular period, will be devoted to transporting at least four employees between their residences and the place of employment.

Employer-Provided Transit Passes

Still another way to provide an employee with a fringe benefit for transportation to and from work is to provide a transit pass. Up to certain limits, these fringes are excludable from income by the employee. A transit pass is any of the following:

♦ A pass

♦ A token or fare card

♦ A voucher or any other item used for transportation or for a reduced transportation rate

Further, the transportation must be on mass transit facilities such as by rail, bus, or ferry.

Key Observation: Cash reimbursements to employees for transit passes do not generally qualify for the same tax-free treatment unless it can be shown that such passes were not readily available for distribution by the employer.

The Dollar Limitation of Transportation Fringe Benefits

There is a dollar limitation on the amount of qualified transportation fringe benefits that can be considered tax-free. The amount of qualified fringe benefits that an employee can exclude from income is based on the type of benefits provided.

♦ For qualified parking the maximum tax-free amount is limited to $190 (up from $185 in 2002) per month.

♦ The tax-free amount for employer-provided transit passes and commuter transportation in commuter highway vehicles (combined) is $100 per month.

◆ The dollar amounts of these limitations are to be increased each and every year based on a prescribed index reflecting cost of living adjustments.

Special Note: An employer can elect to pay for and deduct transportation fringes in excess of these limitations, even though the tax-free portion to the employee is limited to these amounts.

The De Minimis Fringe Benefit

Just like it sounds, a *de minimis* fringe is an insignificantly small benefit made available to an employee. In fact, it is small enough in dollar value that the IRS will not bother to require the employee to report it. After considering the frequency with which these benefits are made available, the *de minimis* rule suggests that it wouldn't be worth the effort for IRS to try and account for them.

Special tax-free treatment can apply to *any* property item or service that an employer might make available to employees during their course of employment. The following are some common examples of tax-free *de minimis* fringes as spelled out in the tax regulations:

◆ Occasional typing of personal letters by a company secretary

◆ Occasional personal use of an employer's copying machine

◆ Occasional cocktail parties or theater or sporting event tickets

◆ Group meals or picnics for employees and their guests

◆ Traditional birthday or holiday gifts with a low fair market value, not including cash

◆ Coffee, doughnuts, and soft drinks

◆ Local telephone calls

◆ Flowers, fruit, books, or similar property provided to employees under special circumstances, such as illness, outstanding performance, or family crisis

The tax law spells out certain specific benefits that *do not* meet the definition of *de minimis* fringes and thus are fully taxable. These include the following:

◆ Season tickets to sporting or theatrical events

- Commuter usage of an employer-provided automobile more than one day a month
- Membership in a private country club or athletic facility, regardless of the frequency with which the employee uses the facility
- More than $2,000 employer-provided group term-life insurance on the life of the spouse or child of an employee
- Use of an employer-owned or leased facility for a weekend

Key Observation: Although the above items are normally taxable, some may enjoy tax-free exclusion as a fringe benefit under some other provision of the law, such as a working condition fringe.

You must evaluate the frequency with which fringe benefits are made so that you can determine if the benefits are truly *de minimis* in amount. You need to look at the frequency that you, as the employer, provide the fringe benefit to each of your employees. Accordingly, the rule states that if an employer provides a free meal every day to one particular employee only, the value of those meals is not *de minimis* with respect to that employee—even if the meals are provided infrequently or occasionally to the entire workforce.

Q. Do cash payments and cash-payment equivalents qualify for tax-free treatment under **de minimis** fringe benefit rules?
A. Generally, neither cash payments nor gift certificates qualify as **de minimis** fringes. For example, if you provide one of your employees a single ticket to a popular new theater event, the employee can exclude the ticket as a **de minimis** fringe. If you give the employee cash to purchase the ticket, it is **not** tax free.

There are essentially two exceptions in which an employee can receive a cash payment or allowance and have it treated as a *de minimis* tax-free benefit:

- meal money
- local transportation fare

For meal money or local transportation fare to be excludable as a *de minimis* fringe, they must not only be reasonable but also meet the following conditions:

- They are provided on an occasional basis, not regularly or routinely.
- They are due to overtime work.
- They are for meals and meal money that enable the employee to work overtime.

How to Qualify Payments for Local Transportation as a De Minimis Fringe

The tax-free benefit for local transportation is only available when the transportation is provided because of *unusual* or *unsafe* conditions for the employee.

Unusual circumstances are determined on a case-by-case basis to determine if the employee is entitled to exclude the benefit from income. Some examples that qualify include the following:

- A normally 9-to-5 employee is called in for a special project at 8 P.M.
- An employee is asked to temporarily change a day shift routine to a night shift for a one-week period.

A Cafeteria Plan

A cafeteria plan is the one employer-sponsored plan in which the employee is actually given a choice between taking cash or certain specific tax-free fringe benefits. Under ordinary circumstances, whenever an employee has a right to choose between nontaxable and taxable benefits, such as cash, that right causes a taxable event regardless of the decision.

However, under a cafeteria plan, no amount will be taxable to the employee who chooses among the fringe benefits in the plan. There will only be taxable income if the employee happens to choose the cash as payment.

With a little bit of planning, the employees can lower their taxable income while tax-deductible contributions continue to be made by the employer.

Qualifying fringe benefits in this context include the following:

◆ Medical insurance reimbursement plans

◆ Group term-life insurance

◆ Dependent care assistance plans

◆ Disability plans

◆ Transportation and parking benefits

◆ Contribution to a qualified 401(k) pension plan

Illustration 6.10

BB Corporation pays Lois, an employee, $40,000 annually, plus $6,000, which she is free to take in cash or in qualified benefits.

If Lois takes the cash, the full $46,000 will be taxed to her as salary.

If the $6,000 was offered as a choice between cash and benefits under a cafeteria plan, Lois could elect to take the fringe benefits tax-free.

For example, Lois might elect to take medical insurance coverage.

The portion of Lois' salary that is applied toward the medical insurance premiums is excluded from her income. If an employee like Lois later receives insurance reimbursements under the policy, those reimbursements are also tax-free.

To qualify as a cafeteria plan, which could benefit the employee and his or her family, follow the criteria outlined below.

◆ All participants must be regular employees. If only one participant is a nonemployee, then the entire plan would be disqualified, and all benefits would be fully taxable to everyone.

◆ The participants can choose between two or more benefits consisting of cash and qualified fringe benefits.

◆ Participants must first make an election among the benefits offered under the plan.

◆ A cafeteria plan must be in writing and contain certain minimum information.

◆ A cafeteria plan may not provide for deferred compensation arrangements for the participants, except for certain 401k plans.

Key Observation: The purpose of requiring the plan to be in writing is to formalize the plan and eliminate any questions as to its scope and qualifications as a cafeteria plan. The written document must contain data such as a specific description of each of the benefits available, eligibility rules for participation, procedures governing the elections of the employees, and other data on how employees can make contributions under the plan.

Caution! Benefits are also subject to discrimination testing.

Chapter Summary

There are numerous tax-free benefits to expenses you incur as the employer. As long as you follow the IRS rules, a definite tax advantage could emanate from employer-provided

◆ meals and lodging,

◆ dependent care assistance,

◆ services that would be no additional cost to either party,

◆ transportation and trips, and

◆ parking and commuting expenses.

In addition, today's small business owner-employers can use the *de minimis* fringe and cafeteria plan to benefit themselves and their employees while at the same time providing a nice tax shelter for their business expenses.

As with any other business deduction, the IRS will hold you accountable for proper documentation. And, unless you follow these rules, the IRS will place a stringent limitation on these deductions based on a percentage of their adjusted gross incomes.

The key, then, is to set in motion tax-saving strategies that will provide a tax benefit for both you and your employees. The next chapter will provide the techniques for making your employees' business expenses deductible.

7

Steps to Ensure Employee Business Expense Deductibility

INCE 1986, CONGRESS'S QUEST TO TAKE AWAY EMPLOYEES' RIGHTS TO claim tax deductions for business expenses has been relentless. It began with a technique called the 2 percent floor, originally introduced to the 1040 tax return preparer. The average taxpayer discovered the sudden disappearance of the familiar "miscellaneous deductions" category. Miscellaneous deductions had been the general category used when writing off employee business-related expenses. Illustration 7.1 demonstrates the financial limitations imposed on the business professional.

Illustration 7.1

Reedy, an executive with Family Business Corporation, is paid $80,000 annually — his adjusted gross income (AGI). Reedy incurs business travel expenses totaling $1,500, which he pays out of his own pocket.

By applying the 2 percent limitation rule, the first $1,600 of business expense is not deductible.

Although only $100 short of the minimum requirement, Reedy is allowed no business deduction. All of his out-of-pocket costs are wasted for tax purposes.

Now, as business professionals advance to higher income levels, another limitation has been imposed on employee deductions. This limitation places a *3 percent floor* on *all* of the itemized deductions that can be claimed on a tax return.

Special Note: For 2003, any taxpayer whose 2003 adjusted gross income reaches $139,500 or $69,750 if married but filing separately will lose an additional 3 percent of his or her deductions. Although there is relief on the way with this tough 3 percent limitation, it will not be totally eliminated until 2010.

To understand the importance of getting around the limitations, the employer and the employee both need to reflect on the breadth and variety of the business deductions that are lost when they are paid out of the employee's pocket.

The following items are examples of employees' business deductions that generally are wasted as tax write-offs because of the limitations on miscellaneous deductions:

- Business transportation costs
- Commercial travel
- Lodging while away from home
- Business meals and entertainment
- Continuing education courses
- Subscriptions to professional journals
- Union or professional dues
- Professional uniforms
- Job-hunting expenses
- Investment expenses

However, you can take steps to keep deductions for these valuable business expenses, as we'll examine in this chapter.

If you incur business-related expenses as an employee, consider a reimbursement plan option to maximize tax savings.

The First Step: Set Up a Reimbursement Plan

If appropriate procedures are followed, the otherwise wasted business expenses paid for out of the employee's pocket may become fully deductible

Q. What can be done to remove these tough limitations on legitimate business expenses?

A. To remove these limitations on legitimate business expenses, consider setting up a reimbursement plan. If you pay business expenses out of your pocket from time to time and the company cannot afford to reimburse those extra costs, consider reducing your salary by the amount of those business expenses and letting the company pick up the tab. The result could be a 100 percent tax deduction for expenses that would otherwise be lost.

Illustration 7.2

Mark has an adjusted gross income of $100,000. He spends $600 for professional books and supplies and $1,200 for business travel.

Mark will get no deduction, because his business expenses do not exceed the 2 percent limitation of $2,000, or $100,000 multiplied by 2 percent.

However, suppose Mark arranges for the company to reimburse him for the business expenses of $1,800 while reducing his salary for the same amount.

The expense, thus, is passed off to the company, and Mark will succeed in gaining a 100 percent tax deduction.

As an added benefit, Mark will have eliminated unnecessary FICA and other payroll taxes.

There are a few rules that have to be followed to get the tax advantage. Specifically, the company needs to follow the requirements of a qualified reimbursement arrangement. If this is done, any reimbursements or expense account allowances received by Mark need not be reported on his tax return.

The idea is that, with qualified reimbursement arrangements, any reimbursements or expense allowances simply do not have to be included in the employee's income. When this occurs, there is no concern about deductions or limitations because the employee doesn't report the amounts as income in the first place.

In the next section, examine another, more subtle benefit for using a reimbursement arrangement with your employer.

The Second Step: Minimize IRS Scrutiny

In setting up a reimbursement arrangement, the function of taking tax deductions is shifted from the employee to the employer. Many see this as a clear advantage for the business professional because there will probably be less scrutiny under IRS enforcement policy.

Every time you decide to write off your out-of-pocket business expenses on your own personal return, you are making a tactical decision that might trigger something more than a reduction in your tax bill. You were made aware in Chapter 5 that if you include any special deductions on your *personal 1040 tax return,* you may be raising your DIF scores. When those deductions are high enough to qualify as a worthwhile tax savings, your chances of being called in for an audit are raised measurably.

It is a well-accepted fact that an IRS audit will create an additional cost to you as a taxpayer. You may be the most honest taxpayer around, as well as the best record-keeper, but if you are called in for an audit it will invariably cost

- ◆ time to organize your records for the auditor and
- ◆ money to secure professional representation.

When the *employer* is taking legitimate tax deductions for everyday business expenses, there is little reason for the IRS to take issue. On the other hand, if the *employee* is taking deductions for various out-of-pocket business expenses on her or his individual tax return, chances are the red flags will be raised.

Illustration 7.3

Tess was paid a salary of $60,000 from Tessco, a company she manages and partly owns.

She paid, out of her own pocket, $1,500 for auto expenses and $500 for continuing education.

Tess lost $1,200 of her business deductions when she filed her tax return because of the 2 percent limitation, or $60,000 multiplied by 2 percent. Tess also lost some sleep because she feared possible IRS scrutiny. It happened that she had some trouble locating all of her backup records for the expenses claimed and, with her raised DIF scores, she thought a tax audit would be highly likely. If an audit did occur, she was fearful that there might be questions about certain personal "gifts" she received from outside parties. Although her accountant had convinced her that the gifts were totally tax-free, she was convinced that an audit could only lead to embarrassment and a no-win situation.

> The chances that Tess would be audited would have been greatly reduced if she had participated in a reimbursement plan.
>
> Tessco, for instance, could reimburse Tess for her out-of-pocket expenses, then proceed to write off the auto and education expense along with the rest of its ordinary business expenses.
>
> With the business reimbursement plan, Tess would have no raised DIF scores, and the $2,000 in business expenses would be fully deductible.

The Third Step: Choose Between an Accountable Plan or a Nonaccountable Plan

As noted earlier, a reimbursement arrangement needs to meet certain criteria before you can be assured that the payments you receive as an employee are tax-free. You have probably guessed by now, the primary criteria for a reimbursement arrangement must involve some kind of requirement of accountability.

Special Note: The key to getting approval of your employee expenses arrangement from the IRS is to show that you have an accountable plan with your employer.

In an *accountable plan*, the tax benefits are automatic. However, with a *nonaccountable plan*, the employee will

- ◆ be required to report any reimbursements as income;
- ◆ be required to deduct the expenses on personal returns, which will be subject to closer IRS scrutiny; and
- ◆ be subject to the tough floor limitations.

Key Observation: With nonaccountable plans, reimbursement payments must be reported as wages on the **Form W-2** and be subject to withholding and other payroll taxes.

There are no particular formalities for setting up a proper accountable plan and making it work. However, many employers have hastened to draft official policy statements and employment agreements so as to show good faith that the following three specific requirements to qualify an expense reimbursement plan as accountable have been met:

1. There must be a business connection for the expenses.

2. The employee must adequately substantiate expenses to the employer.

3. The employee must return to the employer, within a reasonable time, any amount paid under the arrangement that exceeds the expenses substantiated.

Caution: An employee reimbursement plan can generate attractive savings but you must follow the three simple rules.

The First Condition of Accountability: The Business Connection

The first condition of accountability is an easy one to satisfy when trying to render the reimbursement plan accountable. Illustration 7.4 shows that the expenses have been incurred in connection with the performance of services as an employee.

Illustration 7.4

Richard is a sales agent for Company Z; he incurs expenses for business lunches with prospective customers.

Because business promotion is expected in his position as a sales representative, Richard is performing a specific business function, which is directly connected with his business position.

Thus, the first condition of expenses having a business connection is easily satisfied, and Richard is allowed to exclude the reimbursement from income entirely.

Special Note: If advance payments are made to the employee, they need to be made within a reasonable time of the date it is expected that the expense will occur. Otherwise, that advance will not be treated as meeting the **business connection** requirement.

The Second Condition of Accountability: Substantiation

Whether you plan to have an expense reimbursement arrangement with your employees or not, be aware of the substantiation rules.

Key Observation: If a current expense reimbursement arrangement exists, an agent will look again to your business records. An IRS auditor will require substantiating evidence that the employee provided you, the employer, with the backup data.

An accountable plan exists when the employee accounts for business expenses to the employer. In an accountable plan, when an employee incurs a business expense and seeks a tax-free reimbursement from the employer, sufficient information is needed.

◆ First, the employer must be able to identify the specific nature of the expense item.

◆ Second, it must be shown that the expense is attributable to the employer's activities.

There is a slightly different twist for applying the substantiation rules when an employee expense reimbursement plan is in effect. With such a plan, the employee deals directly with the employer. The plan provides the employer with the prescribed documentation in support of the business expenses incurred.

Working on the "honor system," both parties make a record of the documentation without IRS involvement. The unique twist is that the employer unwittingly takes over the task of tracking the authenticity of the business expenses paid by staff employees directly and alleviates much of the IRS's work.

Like it or not, the employer now has the responsibility of verifying that the substantiation rules have been properly followed before a tax-free reimbursement is made. On the positive side, once the employer is satisfied with the substantiation, the employee may walk away with the reimbursement and no hassles from the IRS.

Remember, each element of expense must be individually substantiated. It is unacceptable for an employee to combine a batch of expenses in general categories like "miscellaneous expense" or "entertainment." Individual details must be directly spelled out by the employee just as if dealing with the IRS directly. An example of individual substantiation is described in Illustration 7.5.

Key Observation: There are special substantiation rules when the reimbursement is for travel, entertainment, gifts, or use of an auto or other listed property.

Illustration 7.5

Faye pays out of her own pocket a printing fee for a company newsletter.

Faye provides her employer with a paid invoice, a written voucher describing the specific business purpose of the newsletter, and a memo showing that the expense was attributable to Faye's employment activities.

Faye has properly substantiated the expense, and thus, the reimbursement is properly excluded from her income and her W-2 reporting.

If the plan reimburses the employee for travel, entertainment, gifts, auto expenses or listed property items, there must be extra proof provided to pass the substantiation requirements. It is important for the small business owner to be familiar with these special substantiation rules for two reasons.

1. Employers will need this more detailed backup data whether they are reimbursing an employee or simply incurring the expenses on their own.

2. This special category of business write-offs is always subject to special scrutiny by IRS examiners because of the frequent abuse with these specific deductions.

Special Note: Because of the IRS's major interest in these special expense areas, the substantiation rules are outlined separately in Chapter 8.

The Third Condition of Accountability: Excess Reimbursement Returned to the Employer

When the IRS set up this final condition for an accountable plan, it wanted to make certain that excess reimbursements were promptly returned to the employer. For example, if the employee receives a reimbursement in excess of the amount that was substantiated, the extra must be paid back within a reasonable period. If not, that excess amount will be treated as paid under a nonaccountable plan.

Remember, with a nonaccountable plan, any such reimbursement will be fully taxable to the employee. Unless the employee can beat the tough floor limitations, he or she can lose the entire tax deduction.

Q. What is the reasonable period of time that the employee has to return the excess amount of reimbursement or provide the substantiation?
A. The prescribed reasonable period of time depends on the method of payment of the expense reimbursement. Generally, the time period runs from 30 to 120 days.

Illustration 7.6

On June 1, Roy paid out-of-pocket expenses totaling $1,900 for professional tools in connection with his job with Fry Corporation.

On the same day, Fry reimbursed $1,900 to Roy.

Roy had lost part of his records—receipts and paid invoices—and was unable to substantiate $700 of the $1,900 in expenses.

By December 1, Roy had not repaid the excess payment nor provided the lost records.

The $700 excess payment was deemed to be a reimbursement in connection with a nonaccountable plan.

Roy was required to report the $700 payment as income for the year. He is entitled to take a corresponding personal deduction for the expense only if he finds the missing records and is able to exceed the floor limitations.

Chapter Summary

In summary, there are two distinct advantages for setting up an employee expense arrangement.

1. Valuable tax deductions that would otherwise be lost due to tough limitations on the individual's tax return are saved.

2. Attention is shifted away from the individual taxpayer to the employer—the business entity. Thus, there is less likelihood for a confrontation with the IRS.

Because this book is directed to small business owners, many are probably wondering if there are any special risks when the employee and the employer are one and the same. It seems illogical, for example, that the IRS would be disinterested in an arrangement whereby small business owners are themselves accountable for all of their own travel and entertainment expenses.

A special provision in the law deals with employees who happen to have an interest in the business. The employee may still be accountable for personally incurred business expenses when the employee owns more than 10 percent of the business. What this means is that the owner-employee needs to be prepared to produce the backup records for the IRS in an audit situation.

As a practical matter, however, this requirement should create no significant additional burden for you. As with any employee who renders an accounting to the employer, it is commonly expected that the employee would keep a photocopy of the substantiation records turned over to the employer. After all, if an IRS agent started investigating the employer's books and found a poorly kept record-keeping system, the employee would be held accountable for the expenses anyway.

Key Observation: Since the new reimbursement rules began, the IRS has rarely challenged their tax-saving benefits. As long as the reimbursement amounts are reasonable in amount, examining agents will usually not quarrel with a company for taking business deductions for expense reimbursements to any employee. The added advantage is that the employee's personal tax return is left alone when a reimbursement plan is in proper working order.

8

Learn How to Beat the Record-Keeping Game

I N THE PREVIOUS CHAPTER, YOU LEARNED THAT SINCE 1986, THE PLAYING FIELD has been changed for individual employees who incur business or professional expenses of any kind. Nowadays, if employees incur costs for such expenses, the tough new floor limitations will eliminate most of the tax benefits.

Through a special plan known as a reimbursement arrangement, employee business expenses become the employer's responsibility, which permits the employee to secure the full value of the tax deductions. By properly accounting to the employer for an expense, the reimbursement doesn't have to appear on the employee's *W-2* or tax return.

The warning, however, is that the procedure doesn't let you off the hook for keeping records of the expenses. The only difference is that the records are usually presented only to the employer rather than to the IRS—a more palatable requirement indeed.

In this chapter, you will learn the rules of the record-keeping game, also known as substantiation rules.

The Burden of Proof Is Usually on You

At one time or another, business owners can expect that they will be challenged by the IRS about their deductions. If your business deductions are challenged, you should be prepared to show that

◆ you are the one entitled to take the deduction in question;

◆ the year for which the deduction is claimed is the correct year; and

◆ the amount claimed is deductible under the law.

Unless you take certain specific steps (identified in Chapter 1) you'll find that the burden of proof is on you for proving your deductions. *Don't take business deductions for granted.* The arguments that "everybody is doing it" or "it's commonplace for a certain expense to be claimed" are not sufficient. Business deductions are a matter of legislative grace; therefore, as a business owner you must establish your right to claim them. If your day of reckoning comes, be prepared to prove that you are entitled to the write-off.

Remember, shortcuts and sloppy record-keeping could cost you big time with lost tax deductions.

On the other hand, the IRS examiners and the courts have been known to allow some leeway for deductions even when the taxpayer has not maintained a sophisticated record-keeping system. As a business owner, you are given the opportunity to provide corroborating evidence or testimony to support the burden of proving that the expense was in fact a true business expense.

Remember, when no reliable testimony or evidence is presented by taxpayers, the IRS has consistently denied the authenticity of the business expense claimed.

Illustration 8.1

Ned owns a small design company, Nedco. Last year he failed to keep records for the cost of its materials and tools.

Upon IRS audit, Ned managed to produce a detailed schedule for many of the materials and tools by using trade catalogs as guides for description and pricing.

The catalogs, however, were not identified or brought into evidence. He did not present data about the alleged suppliers or other outside testimony either.

Nedco was prohibited by the IRS from deducting the cost of the materials and tools. If outside testimony or objective evidence had been provided, the deduction might have been allowed.

Special Note: It is up to you, the taxpayer, to take the initiative and provide all necessary documentation to support a claim. Contemporaneously written notations, statements from witnesses, and any reliable reference material all have major relevance when taken as a whole.

Claim Your Deductions in the Right Year

One common problem taxpayers face comes from their failure to claim business deductions in the proper year. Each tax year is handled separately and apart from other years. The IRS is very scientific in ensuring that no income or expenses are pushed in a year that they were not incurred.

If you incur occasional out-of-pocket cash expenses in your business, keep a detailed daily log. Even if the expenses are for minor items like telephone calls, tips, or tolls. Keep a written record detailing the amount, date, and purpose.

Illustration 8.2

Joann, a management consultant, paid for the lease of computer equipment during her first year of business.

Since her income was negligible that year, she didn't claim the rental expense.

She did, however, take the deduction in the following year when her tax bracket was much higher.

Joann is not entitled to the deduction in the second year. In the event of an IRS audit, she could be subject to a tax assessment, including interest and penalties.

Pay by Check

Oftentimes, small business owner-operators are unable to produce canceled checks in support of the expenses claimed in their business operations. The best way to prove the existence of a business expense is to *pay by check.*

If you have a business deduction and are uncertain as to which of the two consecutive years it belongs, choose the earlier year. If the IRS takes issue, you can move the deduction to the following year. If you start by taking it in the latter year and it is not approved, then you may be prohibited by the statute of limitations from claiming it in the earlier year.

There are many excuses why check-writing is not always practical. You might reason that the $5 purchase of some cleaning materials, or the occasional $2 parking meter fee is easier to pay by cash. Truly, not everything can be paid directly by check in business.

However, use your checkbook as the ultimate backup weapon anyway. When you have occasional out-of-pocket cash expenditures, jot down the details on a petty cash voucher. At least once a month, write a business check to reimburse yourself for those monthly cash expenditures. This provides a formal basis for the simple entries that you enter on your books. This procedure provides timely corroboration and evidence for the expenses and gives a more business-like appearance for the management of your overall accounting records. Refer to Chapter 7 for the rules on expense reimbursement arrangements.

There is no law that states you can't pay your bills in cash. If you must pay a bill with cash, be prepared to take a few extra steps to prove the existence of the business expenditure.

As might be expected, IRS agents become particularly inquisitive when observing that there are significant cash transactions in a business enterprise. Whenever they find owner-operators not making their business expenditures in the normal check-writing fashion, they always begin to broaden their investigation and ask more questions.

Prove the Legitimacy of Cash Expenditures

It is quite common for an IRS examining officer to blatantly disallow certain business deductions because the taxpayer did not have a typical accounting system. It is even more common to challenge deductions when expenditures are not supported by the usual canceled checks. However, in numerous cases, IRS findings have been overturned and the record set straight for the taxpayer in the appeals process. This means the IRS cannot dictate that the canceled check is the only documentation available to prove the authenticity of a business expenditure. Illustration 8.3 explains what is necessary to prove business expenditures have been made.

Illustration 8.3

Rick is a business owner who made cash purchases of inventory. Rick produced detailed invoices signed by the sellers.

The IRS auditor disallowed **all** the purchase deductions, because he was unable to locate any of the sellers.

The court, however, overturned the IRS's insinuation that Rick had fabricated the cash purchases. As a credible witness, the company bookkeeper supported the reliability of the expense claim. Also, the books and records were clear, complete, and kept in a business-like manner.

Illustration 8.4

Rick's brother, Tony, is a business consultant. When the IRS asked for proof that he made the payments for office rental claimed on his return, he could not produce canceled checks. Tony did produce some receipts for the payments, which were signed by the building manager.

Tony was criticized by the court, which was concerned that a professional business consultant would fail to keep canceled checks.

Fortunately for Tony, the signed receipts were deemed to be adequate by the IRS. Tony was ultimately allowed the claim for the rental deductions.

As you may see, each case is based on its own merit. When checks are not available, no specific guidelines exist as to what the IRS or the courts will accept as adequate corroborating evidence.

Caution: Only pay by cash when it is absolutely necessary. It pays to look business-slike.

Track All Business Mileage and Telephone Usage

Probably one of the most common record-keeping problems of business taxpayers is substantiation of business mileage.

In one well-publicized case, an Amway® distributor's mileage record could not be tied to the daily business calendar and other activity records. Further, the taxpayer could not even identify the nondeductible commuting mileage from his residence to the place of employment. "No substantiation, no deduction" was the final message to the frustrated taxpayer.

Remember, travel and transportation are in a special category of business expenses that requires a prescribed format of record-keeping procedures spelled out in the tax law.

Another common problem area involves the business use of your telephone. In another high-profile case, a sales representative failed to meet certain common sense rules of substantiation. As others have tried, this taxpayer came up with a round estimate of the business usage on his home phone. With a probably conservative, good-faith estimate, his tax return showed 80 percent of phone calls were exclusively for business activity.

The IRS disagreed. The taxpayer had done nothing to adequately identify on his telephone records the specific nature of any of the individual business calls, and thus, no deduction was allowed. A contemporaneous record detailing the purpose of the telephone calls would have salvaged the deduction.

> **Special Note:** Current tax law stipulates that if you have a single phone line in your home, then the presumption is that all local calls are personal in nature and not deductible.

Pay Close Attention to Detail

As most professional tax advisors will attest, poor record-keeping is one of the biggest roadblocks in the way of successfully representing a client before the IRS. Even if you have canceled checks and have a normal bookkeeping system, extra backup data may sometimes be required to ensure your business deduction.

> **Key Observation:** Often an expense is contested by an examining agent because the taxpayer didn't take a moment to make a brief notation at the

time the expense was incurred. IRS auditors are trained to look well beyond formal journal entries and the standard accounting books for supporting evidence. The following illustrations provide examples of this principle.

Illustration 8.5

Valerie is a property manager who purchases large quantities of business materials. As a responsible business owner, she seems to do everything in line with correct, general bookkeeping procedures.

When Valerie makes a payment, it is reflected on credit card statements, canceled checks, or both.

The payments are neatly organized in a cash disbursements journal.

A formal general ledger exists, giving a concise summary of all operation expenses.

Thus, Valerie's business materials appear to be readily identifiable to the IRS.

If Valerie were audited, the IRS examining officer initially would most likely look favorably at her in terms of general credibility and accuracy.

However, the agent might ask to see some additional backup data if Valerie had purchased unusually large quantities of business supplies. Without additional explanatory data, how would the agent know whether some of the plumbing supplies weren't actually used in Valerie's own kitchen or if check payments to the hardware store had really been Christmas presents for her family?

If Valerie can provide a reference file with written details for each expense item, the examining officer would most likely close the case without raising costly challenges about the deductions.

Illustration 8.6

Henry, an actor, deducted so-called business supplies on his tax return. He kept a logbook to note that the supplies were for skin care, hair care, and makeup.

He did not, however, provide any details as evidence to prove the supplies were for business rather than personal use.

The tax court did not want to be in the position of making the choice, and thus, the deduction was denied.

Illustration 8.7

Julia owned numerous rental properties.

Under audit, she claimed that her personal gardener also took care of her

---

> rental units and that a portion of his cost should be deductible.
> The IRS disagreed. There was no evidence to support the actual time spent by the gardener on each project.

As seen in these illustrations, the absence of supportive written detail can cost a taxpayer the right to make what appears to be a legitimate claim.

When All Else Fails, Get Outside Testimony

Obviously, a businessperson who has complete books and records and additional backup will have little difficulty in proving the deductibility of business expenses. Unfortunately, successful businesspeople can't spend all their time playing bookkeeper. There will be times when they don't have all written records and will need alternative ways to substantiate expenses for the IRS. In those cases, outside testimony can be key.

> **Q.** How far can I go without standard accounting records and detailed memos?
> **A.** The answer usually depends on the amount of evidence presented by your outside witnesses, their general credibility, and any contradictions in the given testimony. Illustration 8.8 demonstrates the importance of witness testimony.

> **Illustration 8.8**
> Miles, a freelance movie producer, spent two years in Africa on an assignment.
> His responsibilities required him to hire a staff to perform a variety of duties, including photography, sound functions, cooking, and automobile driving.
> All Miles' books and records were destroyed by fire.
> After the credible testimony of his staff members, the tax court was satisfied that the deductions Miles claimed were valid. Even though the backup records were not particularly sophisticated, the testimony proved that they did seem to tie into the books.

An Exception to the Rules: The Noted Cohan Case

Named for the famous entertainer, George M. Cohan, this case is often relied on by taxpayers who—for one reason or another—simply cannot prove certain deductions claimed on their tax return. The principle is based upon the court's authority to make a deal with the taxpayer when there is evidence to show that the IRS is probably wrong in denying a deduction.

Herein, a reasonable estimate is made of an expense based on the facts that are available. This subjective approximation is only made when

◆ the IRS denies the *entire* business deduction, or

◆ the amount allowed by the IRS was arbitrarily *low*.

The Cohan method of estimating expenses will only be used when it can be shown that

◆ a business expense must have existed in view of the income that was reported by the business, and

◆ it can be demonstrated that the taxpayer is entitled to the deduction and is able to come up with a plausible basis for making the estimate.

Taxpayers should be aware of the many risks with this approach when trying to secure tax deductions, as explained in Illustration 8.9.

Illustration 8.9

Candice owns a janitorial business. Her accountant lost all of her business records.

Without any documentation, the IRS denied the entire deduction for cleaning supplies she had requested.

The court overturned the decision and allowed Candice her deduction. It stated that the IRS acted arbitrarily in view of the reported income of the business.

It was pointed out that the taxpayer could not have earned her reported amount of income without incurring some expenses for cleaning supplies.

It was also noted that Candice was able to help put together a reasonable estimate based on the facts of the case.

Special Note: There is a common situation, however, in which the courts will readily refuse to give the taxpayer a break by granting any estimated deduction for business expenses. This occurs when the taxpayer was able to obtain duplicate records or other evidence but did not.

101

Small business operators are expected to provide the IRS with whatever books and records were maintained. If the records could be introduced as evidence at a trial but are not, every single operating expense of the business could be denied.

Finally, the following are a special group of business expenses for which the Cohan rule will not apply under any circumstances:

- Travel expenses
- Entertainment
- Business gifts
- A special class of deductions referred to as listed property items

For these particular expenses, estimates are simply not permitted, and the taxpayer must come up with specific proof as detailed in the law. Without this specific proof, no deduction is allowed.

Specific guidelines for deducting this special class of business expenses are outlined in Chapter 9.

Chapter Summary

Shortcuts in record-keeping never pay off for the small business owner. Although recent concessions have made it easier to deduct legitimate business expenses, it is a significant advantage to make a record of as much detail as possible.

9

Different Rules for a Special Class of Deductions

E VERYONE IN BUSINESS TODAY, IN ONE WAY OR ANOTHER, INCURS COSTS THAT involve travel, entertainment, business gifts, or some form of a listed property deduction, such as computers and automobiles. These particular write-offs can generate enormous tax savings for a wide variety of small business owners.

On the other hand, many small business owners fear taking full advantage of these deductions because the IRS closely scrutinizes them. It is easily understood why some owners could be intimidated by the record-keeping requirements for this special class of expenses.

It is tough to survive in today's environment under the juggernaut of rules, regulations, and bureaucratic policies. The last thing a small business owner has time for is more bookkeeping and administrative headaches.

What you can do is learn and adhere to the IRS's substantiation guidelines when you try to claim a deduction for the following special class of expenses:

- ◆ Travel

- ◆ Entertainment and business gifts

- ◆ Listed property deductions—some elements of a special class of business property deductions such as computers and automobiles

This special grouping of expenses, as pointed out earlier, requires strict substantiation guidelines to validate a tax deduction. The Cohan Case in Chapter 8, and any other methods of estimating deductions, won't work when these particular expenses are involved. Keep in mind, if your small business has an expense reimbursement arrangement, there is a different twist on the substantiation rules.

As pointed out in the previous chapter, the reimbursement arrangement has shifted the substantiation requirements for business expenses from the employee to the employer. When there are strict substantiation guidelines, as with this special class of expenses, those guidelines must be met. Only this time, the employee accounts directly to the employer instead of to the IRS.

This chapter spells out the substantiation requirements in the simplest language possible. It will spell out how you could qualify your special class deductions with minimum effort. You will learn your rights in the event that you cannot keep up with the strict laws as they apply to this special class of deductions.

Know the Special Class of Deductions: The Elements of Deductibility

No deduction will be permitted particularly with various travel and entertainment expenses, unless the taxpayer verifies all of the following items for each expenditure:

- ◆ The amount of the expense or item
- ◆ The time and place of the expense, whether it be travel or entertainment
- ◆ The date and description of business gifts
- ◆ The business purpose of the expense or item
- ◆ The business relationship to the taxpayer of each person entertained or receiving a gift

For this special class of expenses, the IRS is looking for solid proof that the expenses were actually incurred. Accordingly, the five specific substantiation requirements must accompany each expense included in these categories. That means some special written memorandums are required.

> **A** simple notebook entry can go a long way to satisfy the tough substantiation rules.

If you don't have a system to make simple explanatory notations, then purchase an inexpensive notebook to make memorandums. Remember, to take advantage of this special class of business deductions, you simply need to create a reasonable record-keeping system. Even if it is an informal method, show that you have taken steps to provide the five specific details as listed above. For instance, a brief journal entry noting the *amount, time, place, date, purpose*, and *business relationship* must be made at—or near—the time the expense was actually incurred.

Illustration 9.1

Barbara entertained a significant number of prospective clients in a real estate development business but feared meeting the tough substantiation tests by the IRS.

Taking the advice of her attorney, she created a detailed information trail by charging **all** entertainment expenses on a business credit card. Under audit, Barbara confidently presented the IRS officer with the credit card statements that efficiently recorded (1) the **amount** of the expense and (2) the **date and place** of the entertainment.

The IRS disallowed her a full deduction because two important elements were missing: (1) the **business purpose** of each lunch and dinner and (2) the **business relationship** of each person she entertained.

Barbara should have made separate contemporaneous notations in a book or on the credit card vouchers. An informal memo identifying the client and the real estate transaction would have sufficed.

As seen from Illustration 9.1, substantiating the business purpose for travel, entertainment, and business gifts is probably the toughest requirement in the prescribed format. Cases abound where the taxpayer's accounting records were deemed inadequate because they did not contain a simple written statement about *why* a business luncheon or a special trip took place.

However, it should be noted that lately, the IRS and the courts have become more reasonable in accepting that the degree of substantiation will vary based on the facts and circumstances in each case. The rules are bent in the substantiation of business purpose in some cases, such as those detailed below.

◆ A written explanation about the discussion that took place is not necessarily required for every business meal paid for by a salesperson who calls on customers in an established sales route.

◆ An explanation was considered self-evident in a case where a certain title company tried to substantiate a number of out-of-state business trips that the title company had sponsored. The company had invited a number of real estate attorneys and various real estate professionals in the community. The taxpayer prevailed because the out-of-state meetings were backed up by minutes of board meetings, advance notices, technical reports, and numerous supporting documents and testimony.

When You'll Need Additional Documentary Evidence

Clearly the best way to get a deduction for this special class of expenses is to keep some kind of account book, diary, or log. In these records you have a complete record of the expenditure at or near the time that it was incurred. There are times, however, when even extensive written memos won't satisfy, and additional documentary evidence will be required to substantiate the expense.

> **Q.** What kind of expenses specifically necessitate that additional documentary evidence, such as receipts and paid bills, must be provided?
> **A.** Generally, documentary evidence is required when the expense is for (1) lodging while traveling away from home and (2) any other separate expenditure of $75 or more.

Interestingly, the requirement to identify in detail nominal amounts has been around for decades. As one more anachronism in the tax code, this floor limitation prompts today's business owner to ask, "Just what business expense wouldn't cost more than *$75* in today's economy?"

Special Note: In spite of the sparse $75 rule, all small business owners should get additional documentary evidence to substantiate **all** business expenditures in the special class of expenses. You probably will find it advantageous to have a signed receipt or a paid bill for all travel, entertainment, business gifts, and listed property items.

Q. What information should the documentary evidence show to substantiate the special class of expenses?
A. All receipts and paid bills must indicate the amount, date, place, and essential character of the expense.

Indeed, the requirement to produce paid invoices and receipts for virtually every expense related to travel, entertainment, business gifts, and listed property deductions is a stringent one. Remember, *anything over $75* requires additional documentary evidence.

Obtain a Collective Voice: Use Corroborated Statements as Backup

As previously stated, the tax law emphatically states that any deduction in the special class of business expenses must be substantiated by adequate records. In that same section of law, you can observe that the deduction could also be substantiated by the employee's own statement if supported by corroborating evidence.

Accordingly, you can take steps to protect your deductions for which there are no records by obtaining backup statements from outside parties. There are two words of caution. First, statements by outside parties must be precise. Second, the corroborative evidence must be either written or verbal statements by individuals with prior knowledge of the element of the expense. When you are trying to prove business purpose or the business relationship of a transaction, the IRS will accept circumstantial evidence.

Where substantiation records are missing or unavailable, the courts will accept verbal testimony from outside parties about the content of the records, provided that the testimony is credible.

Special Note: Self-serving testimony by the taxpayer that is not backed by corroborating evidence is not enough to prove the deduction.

Illustration 9.2

Dr. Eddington is a physician whose practice requires him to travel in and around three counties.

Because of his stressful circumstances, he was unable to keep the required log of his business and personal mileage for last year.

Upon audit by the IRS, Dr. Eddington produced some convincing corroborative evidence, including statements from both his secretary who kept the office records and an emergency room supervisor. He testified on behalf of himself as well.

He also showed that he had documentary evidence as he presented the IRS with office records of house calls, auto service records and mileage summaries.

Dr. Eddington had proved his case with both written and verbal documentary evidence, even though he did not keep a contemporaneous log.

Illustration 9.3

Mary, a real estate agent, incurred expenses for automobile use, meals, and lodging.

The IRS determined that Mary's canceled checks, receipts, and entries in her daybook were not sufficiently detailed to constitute adequate records.

However, she offered sufficient corroborating evidence from outside parties to establish the amount, time, place, description, and business purpose.

This evidence, along with her own testimony about the importance of incurring travel and entertainment in her business was sufficient to prove the deduction.

Illustrations 9.2 and 9.3 show how corroborating evidence from outside parties can win cases for taxpayers. On the other hand, there are numerous cases that have ended with negative results for the taxpayer. Consider Illustration 9.4

Illustration 9.4

Hal presented various kinds of documents to back up business travel and meals with his clients.

He kept checks, restaurant receipts, ticket stubs, and credit card statements.

He did not, however, bring forth evidence of the **business purpose** of each encounter or other verification to substantiate that business discussions actually occurred.

None of Hal's deductions were accepted as substantiated business expenses.

Travel Expense (Away from Home)

Travel expense is an important item to the small business owner because it generally involves a substantial tax write-off and occasionally allows some mixture of recreation with business. To qualify for the deduction you must show the cost was incurred while traveling away from home in the conduct of your trade or business.

All small business owners should be careful not to rely on the idea that there are easy alternative methods for substantiating the special class of business expenses. IRS agents are sensitive to the five specific requirements for proving every element of these expenses.

The broad definition of deductible travel expense includes all costs of travel, including meals and lodging while away from home. These can include the following:

- All transportation involved in a project worked on away from home—this means transportation to and from the location and any transportation costs while you are at that location
- Telephone, telegraph, and fax services
- Computer rental fees
- Baggage service
- Personal laundry, cleaning, and pressing
- Private airplane operation costs
- Maintenance and operating costs of an automobile

IRS examining officers are quick to raise questions about the away-from-home requirement because there is misinterpretation as individuals make various kinds of business trips.

As a business traveler, ask yourself, "How far do I have to travel before my expenses are deductible because they were incurred away from home?"

Remember, there is no set number of miles that need to be traveled. Instead, you must show that your duties required you to be away from the general area of your tax home for a period substantially longer than an ordinary workday. Furthermore, during your time away, you will require sleep or rest to meet the demand of your work. Put another way, your absence from your tax home must be of such duration

Travel expenses for conventions, seminars, and business trips are carefully scrutinized by the IRS to determine if they are merely disguised vacations. If the business or professional activity is only a small fraction of the sojourn, the major part of the deduction, including the cost to get there, will be disallowed.

that you could not reasonably leave and return to that business location before and after each day's work.

Illustration 9.5

Dr. Palmer attends a dental surgeon seminar in Bermuda. The primary reason for the trip is strictly professional.

While in Bermuda, he includes reasonable costs for hotel, meals, tips, laundry, and telephone service.

During his stay, he spends some time sightseeing and touring the city, unrelated to his professional work.

Dr. Palmer can deduct all his costs except for the local sightseeing and touring, which is considered personal enjoyment.

Travel expenses away from home can provide enormous tax savings if you meet the temporary period rule.

IRS ATTEMPTS TO DEFINE TEMPORARY WORK ASSIGNMENT

If you have ever traveled away from home on business, you are surely aware of the significant tax advantage of writing off the cost of your travel-related expenses. Transportation, meals, lodging, and even laundry expenses are among the wide assortment of deductions available that can provide tax savings to a business traveler. The problem, however, lies in ascertaining which of your travel assignments qualifies for the deduction.

In basic terms, to qualify for a deduction, you must demonstrate that the business travel assignment was strictly for a temporary period. Anything beyond temporary travel infers that the travel period was in fact indefinite. In other words, when you don't know how long you will be away from home, you simply aren't entitled to any deduction for your travel-related costs.

In the past, the rules for defining temporary work assignments have been rather complex. The rules were even more complicated when your travel stay extended as much as one to two years. The IRS has tried to clear the air by providing three easier-to-follow guidelines for defining temporary, thus deductible, travel.

If your employment away from home at a single location is realistically expected to last, and does, in fact, last for one year or less, the employment is considered temporary and, thus, is deductible—unless facts and circumstances indicate otherwise. If that period of employment away from home is realistically expected to last for more than one year, the employment is indefinite and, thus, not deductible. This guideline applies whether or not the employment period exceeds one year. If employment away from home at a single location initially is realistically expected to last for one year or less, but at some later date, it is then expected that the time period will probably go beyond a year, then two situations may result. All that time that it was realistically expected that the job assignment would be one year or less will be treated as temporary—thus, deductible. At the point in time that it looks like the job will go beyond a year, you will be then in the *indefinite* zone, which means no more deductibility. Take a closer look at this guideline as described in Illustration 9.6.

Illustration 9.6

Simon took a job assignment in Chicago that was expected to last nine months. Due to new circumstances that occurred after seven months, it became apparent that Simon would be required to stay in Chicago for six additional months — for a total of 13 months.

Simon's employment in Chicago is temporary for seven months, and, thus, his travel expenses are deductible for that period.

During the remaining six months, his stay in Chicago is considered indefinite and not allowable as a deduction.

Obviously, you should clarify job assignment time schedules for yourself and your employees to evaluate the effects of a potential tax trap.

In the event that you are unable to produce the required backup documents, don't necessarily be alarmed. IRS examining officers sometimes give the impression that there are no exceptions to the rules. Be aware that several tax court decisions have disagreed with the IRS and allowed taxpayers to substantiate certain expenses with various types of corroborating evidence.

NEW RULES ON DEPENDENTS AND AMOUNTS

By and large, the general rules on the deductibility of travel expenses remain unchanged since the tax act of 1993. There are, however, two revisions that are worthy of note. The first refers to the cost of having your spouse or other family member accompany you on a business trip. The second has to do with a change in the amount of business meals that can be deducted after the change in the law.

The current law affects dependents' accompaniment during business travel. No deduction is allowed for the travel expenses of a spouse, dependent, or other individual accompanying a person on business travel unless

- ◆ the family member is an employee who works for the person paying the expenses;
- ◆ the accompanying individual has a bona fide business purpose; and
- ◆ the expenses would otherwise be deductible.

Under the old rules, the accompanying individual didn't have to be an employee.

Illustration 9.7

Mr. Thomas, an employee of Tee Company, is accompanied on a business trip by his wife, Mrs. Thomas, who is not an employee of the company.

Mrs. Thomas served a bona fide business purpose with her presence as she assisted her husband. For example, she arranged all of the business meetings and entertaining of clients after hours.

None of Mrs. Thomas' expenses paid by Tee Company are deductible under the letter of the new law, because Mrs. Thomas is not an employee of the one paying the expenses.

The law does not offer a definition of bona fide employee, nor does it define what is meant by business purpose. Accordingly, whether there is a bona fide employee or a bona fide business purpose will have to be determined on a case-by-case basis.

THE LAW AFFECTS BUSINESS MEAL COSTS

Recent updates in the tax law regarding business meals do not change tax deduction policy or procedure. The change is related to the amount allowed to be written off for meals, whether they are for business travel or for entertainment.

Generally, if business meals are substantiated and are **not lavish or extravagant**, they can be deducted from income. However, the deduction is limited to 50 percent of the amount of the expense.

There are certain cases when the tough 50 percent limitation for meals and entertainment expenses does not apply. Following are several important exceptions where a full 100 percent deduction will be allowed:

- Employer-provided meals on the employer's premises, generally when such meals are provided for noncompensatory business purposes
- Company-wide holiday parties providing food, beverages, and entertainment for employees who are not primarily owners or highly compensated employees
- Employer-paid meals and entertainment that are treated as taxable compensation to the employee
- Meals and entertainment provided to the general public for promotional or advertising purposes, including functions such as free concerts or wine- and cheese-tasting exhibitions
- The cost of food and entertainment provided to customers or patrons in the course of business operations, such as the cost of entertainment in the nightclub where an employee works

As a result of the 1997 Tax Act, certain air transportation employees, certain interstate truck operators and interstate bus drivers, certain railroad employees, and certain merchant mariners face an increased deductible percentage for meals that is being phased in according to the following table:

Taxable Years Beginning in	Deductible Percentage
2002 and 2003	65%
2004 and 2005	70%
2006 and 2007	75%
2008 and thereafter	80%

To ensure a deduction for traveling expenses, including meals and lodging, you need to substantiate four specific elements. To pass the test, keep a journal to record the items listed in the following table.

Amount	Jot down the amount of each expenditure as you travel away from home. Include transportation, lodging, and meals. For your own costs of travel, you can group the cost of breakfast, lunch, and dinner into a category called meals.
Time	Record the date of departure and return of each trip away from home. Show the number of days away from home on business.
Place	Record the destination or locality of each business trip. This simply means to make a note of the city, town, or other designation.
Business Purpose	This is the most confusing aspect to most business travelers. Be sure to take a few minutes to make a memo entry in your record describing your business reason for making the business trip. You might make a note of the business benefit expected as a result of the travel.

Recommended format for substantiating travel costs away from home

Compute Deductions with the Optional Method

Many small business owners are not aware of a simplified method for computing the deductible amount of meals, lodging, and incidental expenses while on business travel away from home. Referred to as the *optional method*, this procedure spares the traveler from keeping an inordinate amount of detail on actual expenses while away from home on business. Generally, this special provision applies to regular employees. However, even employers may now use the optional method for meals only.

The amount that is allowed to be deducted under this provision is set in a federal per diem rate table and is revised at

The basic daily meal allowance for business trips within the continental United States is expected to be $40—for certain high-cost areas, the rate can go up somewhat (subject to change).

different intervals. The table permits the taxpayer to use a flat amount for meals and incidentals without receipts.

Truly, the optional method spares the taxpayer from keeping the actual bills and receipts for every meal and incidental expense item while traveling. However, don't forget to record the three other specific elements—time, place, and business purpose of the travel.

Illustration 9.8

Rick, a self-employed architect, has traveled across two states to Mobile, Alabama. He stays there for 10 days trying to develop new business clients.

Unable to collect all the receipts for his meals and other incidental travel costs, he elects to use the optional method. He carefully keeps a diary identifying the whereabouts of each trip, the date, and a note about each prospective new client.

Rick can substantiate $400 for meals and incidental expenses even though he does not have the actual receipts. This is calculated at $40 per day multiplied by 10 days.

Special Note: The cost of virtually all meals, including beverages, is subject to a 50 percent limit under the law—whether those meals are for entertainment or business travel. So, if you elect the short-cut version of the per diem method of record-keeping, the lump sum allowance attributable to meals and incidental expenses will be subject to the tough 50 percent limitation. For this reason, many will want to consider foregoing the optional method and keep a record of the actual costs, which could be greater.

If you have Internet access, you may obtain the federal per diem rates via the IRS Web site (*www.irs.gov*). In addition to these rates, you will find all the publications and forms for your business's tax-planning needs.

Entertainment Expenses and Business Gifts

Deductions for business entertainment are a prime target for IRS agents and other examining officers. It is seen as the tax deduction most often abused by small business owner-operators looking for self-serving tax write-offs. Because of this assumption, over the years, Congress has written some hard and fast qualifying rules that must be met before this unique deduction will be considered.

The qualifying rules for entertainment deductions are sometimes considered absurd in light of the additional demands that they place on business. The attempt by Congress to react to the abuses of a few has put more pressure on all small business owners already inundated by a sea of bureaucratic paperwork.

The tough requirements for entertainment deductions have reached diminishing returns; only a handful of business operators know exactly how the requirements work. In fact, many tax professionals don't bother wading through all the rules with their clients unless they try to claim an inordinate amount of entertainment expenses. Even highly trained IRS agents often refrain from getting involved with the murky fine points of the law unless there are substantial dollar amounts involved.

Key Observation: Entertainment expense is still high on the list of deductions that raise a red flag on business tax returns. When the amount claimed is abnormally high for the type of business involved, there will be a rise in the DIF scores, which will increase the likelihood of that return getting caught up in the audit stream.

The Impact of the Current Tax Law

Always looking for revenue-raising sources, Congress has found a way to control business entertainment deductions without sending IRS auditors to do the work. In essence, Congress slashed the amount that could be deducted in a normal business setting.

Pass the Entertainment Expenses Deductibility Test

Whether you are in a business or an investment setting, you must meet a certain test for deductibility of entertainment expenses.

As with any cost of doing business, the taxpayer must show that the expense is an ordinary and necessary cost of doing business. (See Chapter 5.) In addition, the cost must be *"directly related"* to the active conduct of the trade or business.

With this kind of language, small business owners, tax professionals, and IRS agents constantly debate about deductibility. The solution can only be settled by subjective negotiation.

The rule is: Entertainment is directly related to the taxpayer's business when it can be shown that there was an active discussion aimed at obtaining immediate revenue or that the entertainment occurred in a clear business setting.

Illustration 9.9

Chip, a self-employed management consultant, held numerous cocktail parties and other social events for his business clients and associates.

His daybook and canceled checks indicated that entertainment had taken place, but there were no detailed records identifying active business discussions, nor did he show the existence of a clear business setting.

No deduction was allowed.

Prepare to pass one more test if you want to ensure locking in your entertainment deduction. The *"associated with"* test is your next step to save the deduction, should you fail the "directly related" test.

Key Observation: The "associated with" test allows you a greater degree of flexibility for getting a deduction because it requires only that the entertainment be associated with the trade or business activity. It also states that the entertainment can take place before or after the business discussions.

There is a myriad of possibilities as to what can and cannot qualify as an entertainment expense when referencing the associated with test. A few observations can be made that might pique the interest of the small business owner as a potential tax-saving advantage with entertainment expenses. The entertainment that takes place before or after business discussions could include activities such as

- ◆ business goodwill entertainment in nightclubs,
- ◆ sporting events,
- ◆ theaters, and
- ◆ fishing trips.

Special Note: It is not necessary that you spend more time on business than on entertainment. It is not important that the entertainment and the business discussion take place on the same day, although it is helpful when the business discussion takes place immediately before or after the entertainment. Remember, each case is based on its own facts and circumstances.

If IRS agents and tax professionals have problems with the strict interpretation of the entertainment expense rules, how are you supposed to know what to do? Clearly, the only way you can survive the business entertainment test is to take aggressive action. Make sure to keep a detailed record each time an entertainment event occurs. Use the five specific elements—amount, time, place, business purpose, and business relationship—and win your case.

Just as you learned with travel expense, you need to create a simple chart that will force you—or your employees—to make a contemporaneous record of all the required details of the entertainment transaction.

Special Note: A report document that looks official will command more respect than some scattered notes in the margin of a daybook. Hastily drawn memos identifying the details about entertainment expenses will come across to the IRS auditor as being non-contemporaneous and, more importantly, inaccurate.

In recent years, IRS auditors have begun to recognize that legitimate small business operators can't always pass these strict record-keeping tests. They recognize, however, that they can still substantiate items such as travel and entertainment by alternative methods often backed up by corroborating statements from outside parties. But even if you don't have corroborating statements on your side, remember that you have rights to substantiate your deductions by less orthodox means, however informal.

On the other hand, there is an abundance of cases with the opposite ruling. Because IRS auditors are particularly inquisitive about entertainment deductions, you will be wise to keep a detailed record. Refer to the table, Elements to Prove Certain Business Expenses, at the end of this chapter.

Illustration 9.10
John, a sales representative, incurred substantial amounts of entertainment expenses throughout the year.

The IRS denied his deduction primarily because he did not keep an organized and contemporaneous log to prove the details surrounding every expense.

Upon appeal, John was allowed the deduction, because it was determined that he had, in fact, taken enough steps.

First, he produced canceled checks showing various restaurants and specific individuals who were involved. Second, an informal diary was produced containing the names of customers that he met on certain days and some of the restaurants where entertaining took place.

Third, and most important, he made an effort to record in his diary certain facts stating that business-related issues were discussed.

Item to Be Proved	Substantiation Requirement
Amount	Record the amount of every expense as it is incurred. Incidental expenses, such as taxis and telephones, may be totaled on a daily basis.
Time	The IRS wants to see a record on the date of the business meals or entertainment event. For meals or entertainment, show the date and duration of the business discussion, before or during the event.
Business Purpose	Make a note of the business reason or the economic benefit gained or to be gained. Also, be sure to comment on the nature of the business discussion.
Business Relationship	Make a memo about the party being entertained. Give the name, occupation, and other identifying data that shows the party's relationship to you. If the entertainment was a business meal, you must also prove that either you, or one of your employees, were at the meal.

Recommended format to prove your entertainment expenses

KNOW THE RULES FOR CLUB DUES

For many years, the small business owner has enjoyed full tax deductions for dues paid to country clubs and social clubs—provided the facility was used primarily for the furtherance of business.

Unfortunately, there had been some changes made under the 1993 tax act. For amounts paid after 1993, the new law went so far as to disallow deductions for all club dues. The disallowance applies to all types of clubs, whether they are business, athletic, social, luncheon, or sporting clubs.

Key Observation: Although the underlying club membership dues are no longer deductible, in certain cases, there may be significant tax write-offs available for club expenses. For example, business meals, drinks, and special functions are deductible if they are directly related to or associated with business or business discussions.

Under later rulings, the IRS relented to public pressure over this tough law. The regulation now makes an allowance in certain cases for dues paid to "professional," "civic," or "public service" organizations. Accordingly, if you belong to such an organization for business reasons, you may now claim the cost of membership. Some examples of the allowable organizations cited in the new regulation are

◆ Kiwanis,

◆ Lions,

◆ Rotary, and

◆ Civitan.

This regulation allows deductions for dues for professional organizations, such as

◆ business leagues,

◆ trade associations,

◆ chambers of commerce,

◆ boards of trade, and

◆ real estate boards.

Illustration 9.11
Lorraine, a mortgage broker, paid $4,000 for her annual dues at a country club where she conducts a vast amount of business.
   The annual bar bill of $3,000 was the result of Lorraine's efforts to promote general goodwill for her business. There were also $5,000 in substantiated

receipts for business luncheons for which Lorraine identified individual clients and the business discussions.

Lorraine is permitted to deduct only the cost of the business luncheons, because they were directly related to the active conduct of her business.

Key Observation: Had Lorraine kept a detailed record of the business solicitation activities at the bar—amount, time, place, business relationship, and business purpose—the deduction probably would have been allowed. She would have demonstrated that her efforts involved something more than general goodwill.

WHEN GIVING GIFTS TO CLIENTS, KNOW YOUR LIMIT

Gifts to clients, customers, and business associates are deductible if they are an ordinary and necessary cost of doing business. It is interesting to note, however, that deductions for such gifts are limited to an unrealistic *$25* per recipient. Because of the minimal dollar amount involved, IRS auditors are not particularly finicky when these deductions are claimed. Some examples of deductible business gifts, subject to the $25 limit are

- ◆ the cost of gifts to customers at Christmas by a small manufacturing business,
- ◆ gifts of flowers to customers whose family members were ill or had died, and
- ◆ the cost of magazine subscriptions to clients.

Remember, business gifts are subject to the tough $25 limitation regardless of whether they are made in connection with a good sound business purpose. The actual deduction is limited to $25 for each individual recipient each year. On the other hand, there is not a limitation on gifts made to business entities, such as corporations or partnerships.

Special Note: Although there is usually no limit on the amount of business gifts made to business entities, the limitation will still apply if the gift is clearly intended for the benefit of a particular shareholder, owner, or employee.

> **Illustration 9.12**
> Near Christmas, Ace Printing Company sent a $30 fountain pen to each of its 40 best customers (all individuals).
> Ace can deduct a total of $1,000 ($25 per pen multiplied by 40 customers).
> Ace Printing also has a major corporate client to which it sent a season of professional baseball tickets costing $250.
> The tickets were to be made available to any of the large number of the corporation's employees.
> Since it was clear that none of the tickets were earmarked for the eventual use of any one individual, the entire cost of $250 is deductible.

Listed Property

For this last segment of special deductions, the same ground rules apply. In other words, do your best to record the details of each transaction. If those records are not available, you should start looking for someone outside to back up your claim.

> **Q.** What specifically is this listed property for which I need special substantiation?
> **A.** For the most part, listed property includes the following business property: automobiles and other transportation property; property used for entertainment, recreation, and amusement; and computers or cellular phones.

If you plan to take a tax deduction for any one of these items, be prepared to substantiate the following, by adequate records or by outside testimony:

- the amount and date of each separate expenditure for each item of listed property
- the amount and date of the use of that property for business
- the business purpose for using the property

Without question, the vast majority of items in this listed property category involve business automobiles. In fact, the numbers of cars used in small business today are so great that the following chapter is dedicated entirely to the tax implications. Suffice it to say for now that if you use any kind of business property that falls into the listed property category, keep a contemporaneous log and record the required details. For automobiles, that means a continuing mileage record. (Refer to Chapter 10 for specific details on automobile usage.)

> **Key Observation:** Whether the listed property item you are dealing with is an automobile, an airplane, or a cellular phone, as a small business owner you should keep not only the prescribed detail of its use, but also substantiate related costs, such as lease payments, repairs, and maintenance.

Illustration 9.13

Amy, a country and western singer, leased a computer in her home, which she only used to record songs and to correspond with radio stations.

She failed to keep a running log of the dates and business use of the computer. However, she was able to produce outside testimony that the computer was only used for the furtherance of business as originally claimed.

Amy was ultimately allowed the deduction. Even though she didn't have written records, her own statements were adequately substantiated by corroborating evidence.

Chapter Summary

The primary purpose of this chapter has been to apprise the small business owner about a special class of business deductions that can be expected to come under special scrutiny by the IRS. The inference is that the expenses within this special grouping are so fraught with abuse that they can only be allowed as deductions if they meet certain specific substantiation requirements.

If you, as a business owner, incur costs for travel, entertainment, and business gifts, you will be required to produce records to identify specifics such as amount, time, and business purpose if called in for audit. You learned that if those records are for some reason unavailable, you may still assert your rights to use other alternatives—regardless of what the IRS examiner might suggest. In other words, the small business owner still has the right to secure the deduction by obtaining outside testimony and corroborating evidence.

ELEMENTS TO PROVE CERTAIN BUSINESS EXPENSES

Timely record keeping: You do not need to write down the elements of every expense at the time of the expense. However, a record of the elements of an expense or of a business use made at or near the other expense or use and supported by sufficient documentary evidence, has more value than a statement prepared later when generally there is a lack of accurate detail.

Separating expenses: Each separate payment usually considered a separate expense. For example, if you entertain a customer or client at dinner and then go to the theater, the dinner expense and the cost of the theater tickets are two separate expenses. You must record them separately in your records.

Season or series tickets: If you purchase season or series tickets for business use, you must treat each ticket in the series as a separate item. To determine the cost of individual tickets, divide the total cost (but not more than face value) by the number of games or performances in the series. You must keep records to show whether you use each ticket as a gift or entertainment. Also, you must be able to prove the cost of luxury box seat tickets if you rent a skybox or other private luxury box for more than one event.

Allocating total cost: If you prove the total cost of travel or entertainment but cannot prove how much it cost for each person, you must divide the cost among you and your guests to determine the business and nonbusiness cost. To do so, divide the total cost by the total number of persons. The result is the amount you use to figure your deductible expense for each qualifying person.

Combining items: You can make one daily entry for reasonable categories of expenses such as taxi fares, telephone calls, or other incidental travel costs. Meals should be in a separate category. You can include tips with the costs of the services you achieved. Expenses of a similar nature occurring during the course of a single event are considered a single expense. For example, if during entertainment at a cocktail lounge, you pay separately for each serving of refreshments, the total expense for the refreshment s is treated as a single expense.

Car expenses: You can account for several uses of your car that can be considered part of a single use, such as a roundtrip of uninterrupted business use, by a single record. For example you may make deliveries at several different locations on a route that begins and ends at you employer's business premises and that may include a stop at the business premises between two deliveries. You can account for these using a single record of miles driven. Minimal personal use, such as a stop for lunch on the way between two business stops, is not an interruption of business use.

Gift recipients: You do not always have to record the name of each recipient of a business gift. A general listing will be enough if it is evident that you are not trying to avoid the $25 annual limit on the amount you can deduct for gifts to any one person. For example, if you buy a large number of tickets to local high school basketball games and give one or two tickets to many customers, it is usually enough to record a general description of the recipients.

If you have expenses for	Amount	Time	Place or Description	Business Purpose and Business Relationship
Travel	Cost of each separate expense for travel, lodging, and meals. Incidental expenses may be totaled in reasonable categories such as taxis, daily meals for traveler, etc.	Dates you left and resumed for each trip and number of days spent on business.	Destination or area of your travel (name of city, town, or other designations).	Purpose: For the expense of the business benefit gained or expected to be gained. Relationship: N/A
Entertainment	Cost of each separate expense. Incidental expenses such as taxis, telephone calls, etc. may be totaled on a daily basis.	Date of entertainment (also see business purpose).	Name and address or location of place of entertainment if not otherwise apparent (also see business purpose).	Purpose: For the expense of the business benefit gained or expected to be gained. For entertainment, the nature of the business discussion or activity if the entertainment was directly before or after a business discussion: the date, place, nature and duration of the business discussion, the identities of the persons who took part in both the business discussion and entertainment activity.

Table 9-1. **Further information for documenting certain expenses (continued on next page)**

If you have expenses for	Amount	Time	Place or Description	Business Purpose and Business Relationship
Entertainment (continued)				Relationship: Occupations or other information (such as names, titles, or other designations) about the recipients that shows their business relationship to you. For entertainment, you must also prove that you or your employee was present if the entertainment was a business meal.
Transportation	Cost of each separate expense. For car expenses, the cost of the care and any improvements, the date you started using it for business, and the total miles for the year.	Date of the expenses. For car expenses, the date of use of the car.	Your business destination (name of city, town, or other designation)	Purpose: Business purpose for using this mode of transportation. Relationship: N/A

Table 9-1. **Further information for documenting certain expenses (continued)**

10

Automobile and Local Transportation Expenses

T HE COST OF BUYING AND OPERATING AN AUTOMOBILE IS ONE OF THE MOST common operating expenses of small businesses. Whether you are self-employed or on the payroll of your own business entity, the rules for deducting automobile expenses should be of prime concern to you. These rules, however, are so fraught with hedges and limitations that many business owners often don't know what they can write off. It is important to understand the variables involved with transportation; then plan ahead!

Commuting Expenses

Everyone is familiar with the general rule prohibiting a tax write-off for the cost of commuting between a taxpayer's residence and place of business. Whether you use a bus, train, or taxi to travel to work, the IRS views the expense as strictly personal in nature, and no tax write-off is allowed.

The rules apply even if there is no public transportation available and commuting by auto is your only option. If you are an ordinary employee, the rules are even tougher.

> **Illustration 10.1**
>
> Theresa, an employee, is legally blind and unable to obtain a driver's license.
>
> Because there is no public transportation in her area, she incurs the expense of taxi service for travel to and from her job.
>
> Unfortunately, the court concluded that there could be no exceptions to the general rule. The deduction was denied.

LOCAL TRANSPORTATION

In light of the tough rules on commuting, there doesn't seem to be much hope of deducting local transportation costs that you incur with your personal car. However, there are some circumstances that offer significant tax saving advantages. If you look closely at these advantages, you'll see that the benefits favor the small business owner.

Small business owners need not be shy about claiming expenses for local transportation when they are so entitled. If the transportation is an ordinary and necessary cost of doing business, and it is not considered commuting, take it as a deduction. Further, if the amount claimed is not an unreasonable amount, the auto expense deduction should not raise your DIF scores or the chance of subsequent audit risk.

WORK AT TWO DIFFERENT LOCATIONS

If your job, as an employee, takes you to two or more places during the course of a single day, you can deduct the cost of traveling from one job to another. Keep in mind, the initial commute and the final return are considered commuting and are not allowed.

> **Illustration 10.2**
>
> Roger is an urban planner who is employed by a small consulting company.
>
> On one long-term engagement, he travels 10 miles from home to job site A and gets no reimbursement for mileage.
>
> On the same day, he is required to incur the additional cost of getting to job site B, some 60 miles farther.
>
> Roger can deduct the transportation costs for the additional 60 miles to get from job site A to B.

WHEN THE OFFICE IS AT HOME

Because of the commuting factor, most taxpayers are denied the ability to claim most, if not all, of their expenses for local transportation in connection with their work. The cost of getting to and from the job simply doesn't come into the equation. For some, the mileage tacked onto their cars just for commuting often adds up to the majority of the total miles traveled for the year. Unfortunately, all those miles are wasted for tax purposes.

When your primary business residence is in your home, a different set of rules may apply. You may be able to deduct all transportation costs from the moment you leave the house on business. (Refer to Chapter 11 for how to qualify for an office in your home.)

Key Observation: Many taxpayers operating out of their home automatically believe that the cost of transportation between their first and last stop of the day is, in fact, commuting and not deductible. The IRS held this position in the past; however, the tax courts have looked at it differently. As a result, many taxpayers with home offices have walked away with the full deduction.

Illustration 10.3

Dr. Sprock, a psychiatrist, has an office in his home, which is the focal point of his practice.

He incurs substantial mileage costs going from his home to several hospitals and clinics in the area where he sees patients.

Because Dr. Sprock has established his home as his place of business, his transportation expenses to the various business locations are deductible. The trips are not regarded as commuting.

In an actual case, an attorney who worked as a subcontractor for a law firm had his office in his home. It was ascertained that he performed 90 percent of his work outside the office of the law firm. In an interesting twist, the tax court concluded that his house was his principal place of business and that auto travel between the home office and the law office was fully deductible.

TEMPORARY WORK LOCATIONS

In a landmark ruling involving local transportation expense, the IRS declared that travel between a taxpayer's house and a temporary work location can be allowed as a deduction. Before this ruling, the only time you could write off travel to a so-called temporary location was when the transportation involved travel to a location beyond the general area of the taxpayer's home.

You will recall from Chapter 9 that with travel away from home, there is no allowable transportation deduction unless you travel outside of the area where you live. The IRS's former position was in error. Transportation expenses to temporary job sites are now deductible even if it only involves *local* transportation.

Special Note: If you can show that the temporary trips are to locations other than the usual place of business, they will be permitted regardless of the travel distance.

Illustration 10.4

Dave O'Brien is a management consultant for Bongo Industries.

He normally travels from his residence to any one of a number of client offices each day.

His cost of traveling to those locations on a regular basis would be considered commuting and no tax write-off would be allowed.

However, If Bongo gives an irregular assignment that causes O'Brien to make some temporary trips to the location of a new project, then that travel expense would be fully deductible.

Special Note: The IRS has warned taxpayers against abusing this liberalized rule by claiming deductions between home and an alleged temporary location when no such trips have even taken place. If this occurs, the deductions will be disallowed and penalties imposed.

 If you have filed a tax return that is not closed by the statute of limitations (usually three years) and you could benefit from this ruling on travel to temporary job locations, consider filing an amended return.

Track Automobile Mileage

To avoid the chore of keeping details of all automobile expenses, the taxpayer is entitled to claim a deduction for a fixed mileage allowance—

for 2002 it was 36.5 cents per mile; for 2003 it was lowered to 36 cents per mile. For 2004, the rate goes to 37.5 cents per mile. Regardless of which method is used, there is *no acceptable substantiation* without tracking the underlying miles traveled for business.

Before looking at the techniques for getting the biggest deduction for your automobile expenses, first focus on the job of determining business mileage.

One of the greatest challenges facing accountants and tax professionals is persuading their small business clients to properly track their business mileage. Too many ignore the responsibility, with excuses like the following:

◆ "It's not worth the bother because of the negligible amount involved."

◆ "I'll keep my receipts for gas and maintenance."

◆ "We can easily reconstruct the mileage figure at the end of the year."

In response, you are reminded that automobile expense is within the special class of deductions requiring special substantiation requirements. The five basic elements—amount, time, place, business purpose, and business relationship—must be proved. In this case, the element most difficult to prove is the amount or—better yet—the amount of business use. In addition to mileage, you may also deduct for tolls and parking expenses when incurred for business purposes.

The IRS has flatly declared that the appropriate way to measure business use of an automobile is to prove the business mileage, unless you can come up with another method. In other words, you could have all the necessary gas tickets and repair bills, but if you can't identify the business miles, you haven't proved anything.

Q. What if I don't have any recorded details of my business auto expense, but I know that I used my car at least 50 percent of the time to visit clients?
A. As with any expense in the special deduction category, you do have an alternative. However, you would have to find corroborating evidence or outside testimony to back up your claim for the business miles traveled.

Failure to track your business miles when they are incurred can cost big dollars—not to mention the added risk incurred.

If you are in a situation where you have absolutely no records to support your business miles claimed, you should try to reconstruct a mileage chart. Refer back to a travel itinerary, a daybook, or whatever sources you can find. Remember, you are entitled to use corroborating evidence even if it is your own testimony. If your testimony is not sufficient, then rely on the testimony of an unrelated party.

As a practical matter, IRS auditors and agents are fairly reasonable when examining the business mileage of the small business owner.

Keep a log to identify the location and purpose of all your business trips if you want to eliminate risk later on. If those records are unavailable, begin to reconstruct your business mileage with the best evidence you can find.

They understand that it is quite difficult for everybody to keep a contemporaneous log recording each minute detail every time you use your car.

Further, they know that if you take the issue to court, the court will probably allow at least some amount of deduction based on the evidence made available—including your credibility.

If you appear credible and provide enough facts and details, your chances are good for a reasonable deduction for automobile expense even if your records are lost or unavailable.

Clearly, there are no set allowances and guidelines for *reasonable* amounts of business mileage for certain businesses or professions. Each case is looked at in terms of its own circumstances. Some interesting conclusions were reached in various court proceedings in which the IRS and the taxpayer were in disagreement. Based on such proceedings, an average time usage per profession is highlighted in the following table.

These business-use percentages have been allowed in certain cases. They are not meant to provide any generally accepted guidelines.

Profession/Business	Percentage Allowed
Anesthesiologist or businessperson	39%
Attorney (with two cars, but only used one car)	75%
Another attorney	30%
Auto dealer	70%
Cemetery plot salesperson	80%
Dentist (directed a clinic and made outside calls)	80%
Doctor	75%
Income tax preparer	15%
Owner of rental real estate	20%
Structural engineer	70%
Wholesale fruit and vegetable dealer	50%

Table 10-1. **Percentage of business mileage per total miles**

Calculate Actual Operating Expenses

You may elect a deduction of the actual costs of operating the car for business instead of claiming the flat mileage allowance. The additional burden, of course, is that the owner-operator must produce additional records to substantiate those expenses.

Typical costs for operating a motor vehicle would include the following items:

- ◆ Gas and oil
- ◆ Lease or rental fees
- ◆ Repairs and maintenance
- ◆ Tires and supplies
- ◆ Insurance
- ◆ Depreciation

INTEREST PAID ON CAR LOANS

Generally, if you own a personal automobile, any interest paid on its purchase will be disallowed as a deduction. Under the current law, personal interest expense is simply no longer deductible. If you are self-employed, however, the business portion of the interest paid on your car will be deducted off the top on the business part of your tax return. This demonstrates yet another disadvantage as an ordinary employee who would be allowed little, if any, deduction because of the tough limitations.

> If the owner of the car is your small corporation, then the interest is deductible as an ordinary business expense, similar to any interest paid for business property. For this reason, many businesspeople prefer to purchase their business cars in the corporate name.

Choose the Mileage Allowance or Actual Expenses

The maximum amount of depreciation for each year you own your car is set forth by the IRS and is subject to change each year. Whether you own an $80,000 Mercedes-Benz or a $25,000 Honda, the maximum amount that you could claim for depreciation is severely limited in a prescribed table set by the IRS. That table, which has become increasingly familiar, is shown below:

Period	Maximum Depreciation Allowed
First Year	$3,060
Second Year	$4,900
Third Year	$2,950
Each Succeeding Year	$1,775

Table 10-2. **Maximum amounts allowed for depreciation**

Q. Is the rumor true that you'd be better off by simply forgetting the actual expenses and claiming the flat mileage allowance?
A. Since the government enacted the restrictive rules on auto depreciation, the difference between the mileage allowance and the actual expenses has been significantly minimized. For example, if you have an inexpensive car and your gasoline and maintenance expenses are minimal, your best option may be to take the mileage allowance. Consider all your options. Be sure to project your

deductions over the time period you expect to own the car, rather than just the first year.

Tax Break Alert: Watch for the special one-time bonus depreciation under the new law. Because of an interesting twist brought about by the economic stimulus law, a major increase in the first-year depreciation allowance emerged for many. The benefits of this new law extend to qualified business autos bought during the period by raising the first-year depreciation by a substantial amount—an additional $7,650 on top of the $3,060 shown in the table above.

For example, suppose you purchased a $20,000 car in 2003 for business use only. You traveled 10,000 total miles the first year. By using the flat mileage allowance of 36 cents per mile you would simply deduct $3,600 on your tax return. With the actual expense method, your depreciation deduction alone would be a staggering $10,710 ($7,650 + $3,060), which is about three times the flat mileage allowance. Of course, any other costs for gas, oil, or maintenance would be allowed as an additional tax write-off. Clearly, a major tax savings can be yours by using the actual method.

For the second year, your depreciation bill is still $4,900. Add this amount to your operating expenses, and you will still have a sizable business deduction.

If you own a car that is priced in the $16,000 range, be aware of a further reduction. This occurs when cars used less than 50 percent for business are limited to a depreciation deduction that is based on a conservative straight-line method over five years. For some, this deduction calculates as low as 10 percent of the business portion of the car for the first year.

Key Observation: In the first year, if you decide to use the actual expense method, including accelerated depreciation, **you cannot use** the mileage allowance for that car in a later year. Conversely, if you claim the IRS

Ask about the new law that can enhance your write-off immensely by increasing your depreciation limits if you purchase an electric car (built by an original manufacturer) or an SUV weighing more than 6,000 pounds.

allowance in the first year and later decide to switch to actual expenses, you are forced to use the limited straight-line method described earlier.

When the Car Is Used for Business and Personal Driving

As a practical matter, very few individuals can actually substantiate 100 percent business use. By the time the taxpayer accounts for personal use of the car (particularly commuting), there is usually a sizable amount of the yearly expense that must be carved out. (See *Form 2106* at the end of this chapter.) Accordingly, you must be careful to claim only the allocable portion allowed.

> **Illustration 10.5**
> Charley drove 16,000 miles last year.
>   12,000, or 75 percent, of those miles were driven for business-related purposes.
>   His actual expenses for the year, including depreciation, were $6,000.
>   Charley is allowed to claim $4,500 ($6,000 multiplied by .75).

Leasing vs. Purchasing

There was a time when auto leasing agents would pitch the fantastic tax benefits to be gained by leasing your car. The premise was that when you deduct lease payments for business property, there is usually no hassle from the IRS. Leasing agents used to make the following claims:

- ◆ "You don't have to worry about making allocations for personal use."
- ◆ "Record-keeping is a lot simpler."
- ◆ "All of your lease payments are fully deductible."

Today, the smart small business owner is aware that none of these claims have merit. Instead, you need to be aware of the following:

- ◆ You *do* have to keep mileage records and identify business and personal mileage.
- ◆ It is just as simple to make payments to a bank as to a leasing agency.

◆ By themselves, lease payments are not necessarily fully
deductible.

How To Write off Your Leased Car

First, determine your total mileage for the year—including personal
miles. Then, apply the business percentage to the sum of

◆ the total of your *actual* expenses for the year—including gas, oil,
maintenance, and insurance—but excluding depreciation; and

◆ all of your lease payments for the year.

Remember, when you lease a business car, you should keep all
your records for operating that car during the year. It is interesting to
note that since 1998 you have a new option to use the optional per
mile allowance. However, you probably will be better off deducting the
actual expenses.

You might argue that the limitation on depreciation makes for a distinct advantage for the leasing option because depreciation is never a
factor. After all, you *do* get a business deduction for the lease payment—
at least for the business portion.

Illustration 10.6

Phyllis is a realtor who leases a $25,000 car on January 1, 2003.

She travels 20,000 miles for the year and 15,000 miles, or 75%, are for
business.

Her records show that she spent $2,200 for operating the car and $5,800 in
lease payments — a total of $8,000.

Her deduction is 75% of her total outlay of expenses, or $6,000 ($8,000
multiplied by 0.75).

The IRS settles this argument by setting specific and equal rates for
both higher- and lower-value cars. The IRS provides a table on form
2106 (included at the end of the chapter) that charges you with a dollar amount of extra income based on the value of your car. This amount
from the table is added back to your income and simply offsets a portion of the deduction that you get for those hefty lease payments.

In Illustration 10.6, the value of Phyllis's automobile in the first year
was $25,000. The income adjustment table causes her to account for

an $83 income adjustment for a car of that value. Phyllis must reduce the amount of her deduction for the lease expense by a modest $62 ($83 multiplied by 0.75). Because Phyllis only had to pick up $62 as an income adjustment in her leasing arrangement, this seems generous compared with the restrictive depreciation tables for purchased cars.

LEASING IS STILL A POPULAR OPTION

You may wonder why there still is a surge of interest in leasing and not purchasing business automobiles. The tax advantage is seen in the IRS's income adjustment for leased cars table. Remember, however, Phyllis only had to pick up $62 as an income adjustment in her leasing arrangement in Illustration 10.6.

In earlier days, it was unimaginable how anyone could fare better by leasing his or her car than buying it. Administrative costs alone, built into the lease contracts, should surely outweigh any advantages of getting a vehicle without the problems of ownership. Recent studies show that this may not be the case. A small business owner looking to conserve up-front cash could drive away with a leased car and stay ahead financially at the same time.

The leasing business is a fast-growing industry that operates differently than the world of buying and selling. The uninitiated and uninformed will pay a price for their lack of awareness. At least be familiar with some of the language used in the leasing business. Know the following terms before talking to a leasing agent:

- ◆ *Capitalized cost* is the overall price agreed upon for the car.
- ◆ *Capitalized cost reduction* is the amount of your down payment.
- ◆ *Invoice* is the price that the dealer paid for the car. Remember, many customers are actually beating this price as the manufacturers offer their special rebates.
- ◆ *Depreciation,* unlike depreciation for tax purposes, refers to the difference between the capitalized cost and the value at the end of the lease term.
- ◆ *Subsidies* are special benefits passed on by the automaker— either through a lower interest rate or a guarantee of a higher residual value at the end of the lease.

◆ *Option to purchase* is important if you lease a higher-quality car that you may consider keeping. It gives you the right to purchase the car for the residual value at the end of the lease.

◆ *Residual Value* is the presupposed value at the end of the lease. You get to agree to this value *before* you sign the lease.

Remember, when in doubt, allow your attorney or accountant to look over the lease proposal.

Chapter Summary

Although auto expenses are a common and acceptable business deduction, there are numerous observations to make in order to qualify deductibility—particularly for local business transportation. The flat mileage allowance is arguably the easiest and most sensible option to use; however, it remains extremely important to track your mileage daily.

When considering leasing a car, keep in mind four important "don'ts."

1. *Don't* get caught up in the *monthly payment syndrome*. There are many facts to consider, such as the dealer's mileage allowance, sales taxes, and property taxes. Read your contract in its entirety and make sure that every promise made is put in writing.

2. *Don't* sign a lease for a period longer than you expect to keep the car. Your cost to get out could be prohibitive.

3. *Don't* accept a proposal without comparing the deal with other leasing firms. Shop and compare with at least two or three independent agencies.

4. *Don't* forget to focus on your purchase options and obligations at the end of the lease period. Insist on a closed-end lease, also known as a *walk-away* lease. Your purchase option in a closed-end lease might give you a win-win situation. At the end of the term, if the car is worth more than the fixed price option, you'll have a bargain. If it's worth less, you walk away.

Form **2106**

Department of the Treasury
Internal Revenue Service (99)

Employee Business Expenses

▶ See separate instructions.

▶ Attach to Form 1040.

OMB No. 1545-0139

2003

Attachment
Sequence No. **54**

Your name	Occupation in which you incurred expenses	Social security number

Part I   Employee Business Expenses and Reimbursements

Step 1   Enter Your Expenses

		Column A Other Than Meals and Entertainment	Column B Meals and Entertainment
1	Vehicle expense from line 22 or line 29. (Rural mail carriers: See instructions.)	**1**	
2	Parking fees, tolls, and transportation, including train, bus, etc., that did not involve overnight travel or commuting to and from work . .	**2**	
3	Travel expense while away from home overnight, including lodging, airplane, car rental, etc. Do not include meals and entertainment	**3**	
4	Business expenses not included on lines 1 through 3. Do not include meals and entertainment	**4**	
5	Meals and entertainment expenses (see instructions)	**5**	
6	Total expenses. In Column A, add lines 1 through 4 and enter the result. In Column B, enter the amount from line 5	**6**	

Note: If you were not reimbursed for any expenses in Step 1, skip line 7 and enter the amount from line 6 on line 8.

Step 2   Enter Reimbursements Received From Your Employer for Expenses Listed in Step 1

7	Enter reimbursements received from your employer that were not reported to you in box 1 of Form W-2. Include any reimbursements reported under code "L" in box 12 of your Form W-2 (see instructions)	**7**	

Step 3   Figure Expenses To Deduct on Schedule A (Form 1040)

8	Subtract line 7 from line 6. If zero or less, enter -0-. However, if line 7 is greater than line 6 in Column A, report the excess as income on Form 1040, line 7	**8**	
	Note: If both columns of line 8 are zero, you cannot deduct employee business expenses. Stop here and attach Form 2106 to your return.		
9	In Column A, enter the amount from line 8. In Column B, multiply line 8 by 50% (.50). (Employees subject to Department of Transportation (DOT) hours of service limits: Multiply meal expenses by 65% (.65) instead of 50%. For details, see instructions.)	**9**	
10	Add the amounts on line 9 of both columns and enter the total here. Also, enter the total on Schedule A (Form 1040), line 20. (Fee-basis state or local government officials, qualified performing artists, and individuals with disabilities: See the instructions for special rules on where to enter the total.) . . . . ▶	**10**	

For Paperwork Reduction Act Notice, see instructions.   Cat. No. 11700N   Form **2106** (2003)

Form 2106 for calculating employee business vehicle expenses (continued on next page)

Automobile and Local Transportation Expenses

Part II — Vehicle Expenses

Section A —General Information   (You must complete this section if you are claiming vehicle expenses.)

		(a) Vehicle 1	(b) Vehicle 2
11	Enter the date the vehicle was placed in service	/ /	/ /
12	Total miles the vehicle was driven during 2003	miles	miles
13	Business miles included on line 12	miles	miles
14	Percent of business use. Divide line 13 by line 12	%	%
15	Average daily roundtrip commuting distance	miles	miles
16	Commuting miles included on line 12	miles	miles
17	Other miles. Add lines 13 and 16 and subtract the total from line 12	miles	miles

18	Do you (or your spouse) have another vehicle available for personal use?	☐ Yes ☐ No
19	Was your vehicle available for personal use during off-duty hours?	☐ Yes ☐ No
20	Do you have evidence to support your deduction?	☐ Yes ☐ No
21	If "Yes," is the evidence written?	☐ Yes ☐ No

Section B —Standard Mileage Rate   (See the instructions for Part II to find out whether to complete this section or Section C.)

22	Multiply line 13 by 36¢ (.36)	22	

Section C —Actual Expenses

		(a) Vehicle 1	(b) Vehicle 2
23	Gasoline, oil, repairs, vehicle insurance, etc.		
24a	Vehicle rentals		
b	Inclusion amount (see instructions)		
c	Subtract line 24b from line 24a		
25	Value of employer-provided vehicle (applies only if 100% of annual lease value was included on Form W-2– see instructions)		
26	Add lines 23, 24c, and 25		
27	Multiply line 26 by the percentage on line 14		
28	Depreciation. Enter amount from line 38 below		
29	Add lines 27 and 28. Enter total here and on line 1.		

Section D —Depreciation of Vehicles   (Use this section only if you owned the vehicle and are completing Section C for the vehicle.)

		(a) Vehicle 1	(b) Vehicle 2
30	Enter cost or other basis (see instructions)		
31	Enter section 179 deduction and special allowance (see instructions)		
32	Multiply line 30 by line 14 (see instructions if you claimed the section 179 deduction or special allowance)		
33	Enter depreciation method and percentage (see instructions)		
34	Multiply line 32 by the percentage on line 33 (see instructions)		
35	Add lines 31 and 34		
36	Enter the applicable limit explained in the line 36 instructions.		
37	Multiply line 36 by the percentage on line 14		
38	Enter the smaller of line 35 or line 37. Also enter this amount on line 28 above		

⊕   Form 2106 (2003)

Form 2106 (continued)

Cents per mile: .36	Depreciation %	New Car Max Depr. Amount	Used Car Max Depr. Amount
First Tax Year	20%	$10,710	$3,060
Second Tax Year	32%	$4,900	$4,900
Third Tax Year	19.2%	$2,950	$2,950
Fourth Tax Year	11.52%	$1,775	$1,775
Fifth Tax Year	11.52%	$1,775	$1,775
Sixth Tax Year	5.76%	$1,775	$1,775
Each Additional Tax Year		$1,775	$1,775

Figure 10-3. **2003 tax aspects of auto leasing 50% bonus depreciation (after May 5, 2003)**

Cents per mile: .36	Depreciation %	New Car Max Depr. Amount	Used Car Max Depr. Amount
First Tax Year	20%	$7,660	$3,060
Second Tax Year	32%	$4,900	$4,900
Third Tax Year	19.2%	$2,950	$2,950
Fourth Tax Year	11.52%	$1,775	$1,775
Fifth Tax Year	11.52%	$1,775	$1,775
Sixth Tax Year	5.76%	$1,775	$1,775
Each Additional Tax Year		$1,775	$1,775

Figure 10-4. **2003 tax aspects of auto leasing 30% bonus depreciation (prior to May 6, 2003)**

Automobile Fair Market Value	Annual Lease Value	New Car Max Depr. Amount	Annual Lease Value
$0 – 999	$600	22,000 – 22,999	6,100
1,000 – 1,999	850	23,000 – 23,999	6,350
2,000 – 2,999	1,100	24,000 – 24,999	6,600
3,000 – 3,999	1,350	25,000 – 25,999	6,850
4,000 – 4,999	1,600	26,000 – 27,999	7,250
5,000 – 5,999	1,850	28,000 – 29,999	7,750
6,000 – 6,999	2,100	30,000 – 31,999	8,250
7,000 – 7,999	2,350	32,000 – 33,999	8,750
8,000 – 8,999	2,600	34,000 – 35,999	9,250
9,000 – 9,999	2,850	36,000 – 37,999	9,750
10,000 – 10,999	3,100	38,000 – 39,999	10,250
11,000 – 11,999	3,350	40,000 – 41,999	10,750
12,000 – 12,999	3,600	42,000 – 43,999	11,250
13,000 – 13,999	3,850	44,000 – 45,999	11,750
14,000 – 14,999	4,100	46,000 – 47,999	12,250
15,000 – 15,999	4,350	48,000 – 49,999	12,750
16,000 – 16,999	4,600	50,000 – 51,999	13,250
17,000 – 17,999	4,850	52,000 – 53,999	13,750
18,000 – 18,999	5,100	54,000 – 55,999	14,250
19,000 – 19,999	5,350	56,000 – 57,999	14,750
20,000 – 20,999	5,600	58,000 – 59,999	15,250
21,000 – 21,999	5,850		

For vehicles having a fair market value (FMV) in excess of 59,999, the ALV is equal to (0.25 x the FMV of the automobile + $500.)

Figure 10-5. **IRS annual lease value (ALV) table**

Automobile/Fair Market Value		Tax Year of Lease				
Over	Not Over	1st	2nd	3rd	4th	5th and Later
$18,000	$18,500	$10	$22	$33	$40	$45
18,500	19,000	12	26	39	46	53
19,000	19,500	14	30	44	53	61
19,500	20,000	15	34	50	59	69
20,000	20,500	17	37	56	66	77
20,500	21,000	19	41	61	73	85
21,000	21,500	21	45	66	80	92
21,500	22,000	55	49	72	87	100
22,000	23,000	25	54	81	97	111
23,000	24,000	28	62	92	110	127
24,000	25,000	32	70	103	123	143
25,000	26,000	35	77	115	137	158
26,000	27,000	39	85	125	151	174
27,000	28,000	42	92	137	165	189
28,000	29,000	46	100	148	178	204
29,000	30,000	49	108	159	191	221
30,000	31,000	52	115	171	205	236
31,000	32,000	56	123	182	218	251
32,000	33,000	59	130	194	231	267
33,000	34,000	63	138	204	245	283
34,000	35,000	66	146	215	259	298
35,000	36,000	70	153	227	272	314
36,000	37,000	73	161	238	285	330
37,000	38,000	77	168	249	299	346
38,000	39,000	80	176	260	313	361

Figure 10-6. Inclusion amounts for cars (other than electric) with a lease term beginning in calendar 2003 (continued on next page)

Automobile Fair Market Value		Tax Year of Lease				
Over	Not Over	1st	2nd	3rd	4th	5th and Later
$39,000	$40,000	$83	$184	$272	$326	$376
40,000	41,000	87	191	283	340	391
41,000	42,000	90	199	294	353	407
42,000	43,000	94	206	306	366	423
43,000	44,000	97	514	317	380	438
44,000	45,000	101	221	328	394	454
45,000	46,000	104	229	339	407	470
46,000	47,000	108	236	351	420	486
47,000	48,000	111	244	362	434	501
48,000	49,000	115	251	374	447	516
49,000	50,000	118	259	385	460	532
50,000	51,000	121	267	396	474	548
51,000	52,000	125	274	407	488	563
52,000	53,000	128	282	418	502	578
53,000	54,000	132	289	430	515	594
54,000	55,000	135	297	441	528	610
55,000	56,000	139	304	452	542	626
56,000	57,000	142	312	463	556	641
57,000	58,000	146	320	474	569	656
58,000	59,000	149	327	486	582	672
59,000	60,000	152	335	497	596	688
60,000	62,000	158	346	514	616	711
62,000	64,000	165	361	537	642	743
64,000	66,000	171	377	559	670	773
66,000	68,000	178	392	581	697	805

Figure 10-6. Inclusion amounts for cars (other than electric) with a lease term beginning in calendar 2003 (continued on next page)

Automobile Fair Market Value		Tax Year of Lease				
Over	Not Over	1st	2nd	3rd	4th	5th and Later
$68,000	$70,000	$185	$407	$604	$724	$835
70,000	72,000	192	422	626	751	867
72,000	74,000	199	437	649	778	898
74,000	76,000	206	452	672	804	930
76,000	78,000	213	467	694	832	960
78,000	80,000	220	483	716	859	991
80,000	85,000	232	509	756	906	1,046
85,000	90,000	249	547	812	973	1,124
90,000	95,000	266	585	868	1,041	1,202
95,000	100,000	284	623	924	1,108	1,280
100,000	110,000	309	680	1,009	1,209	1,397
110,000	120,000	344	755	1,122	1,344	1,552
120,000	130,000	378	831	1,234	1,479	1,708
130,000	140,000	413	907	1,346	1,614	1,864
140,000	150,000	447	983	1,459	1,749	2,019
150,000	160,000	482	1,059	1,571	1,884	2.175
160,000	170,000	516	1,135	1,683	2,019	2.331
170,000	180,000	551	1,210	1,796	2,154	2,487
180,000	190,000	585	1,286	1,909	2,288	2,643
190,000	200,000	620	1,362	2,021	2,423	2,798
200,000	210,000	654	1,438	2,133	2,559	2,953
210,000	220,000	689	1,513	2,246	2,694	3,109
220,000	230,000	723	1,589	2,359	2,828	3,265
230,000	240,000	758	1,665	2,359	2,963	3,421
240,000	250,000	792	1,741	2,583	3,098	3,577

Figure 10-6. Inclusion amounts for cars (other than electric) with a lease term beginning in calendar 2003 (continued)

11

Home Office Expense Strategies for the 21st Century

THE HOME OFFICE EXPENSE DEDUCTION IS ONE OF THE MOST MISINTERPRETED and misunderstood areas of the tax law affecting small business owners today. Only a scant few seem to grasp the actual eligibility requirements for the deduction. Fewer know the long-range implications of claiming a deduction for their home office.

Thanks to recent tax reform, this often controversial deduction has proven to be beneficial to many taxpayers. Further, your home office doesn't have to be your house. It could be a condominium, an apartment, a mobile home—or even a boat.

Pass the Primary Test

It is now confirmed that to claim a deduction for home office expense, you must show that the area in your home was used *exclusively* and on a *regular basis* as

- ◆ the principal place of your business or
- ◆ the place you deal with your clients, patients, or customers in the normal course of business.

IRS agents are quick to take issue with the *exclusive-use* test. Some

If you do use a portion of your residence for business, remove all nonbusiness-related items. Although not essential, you might consider physically separating these office quarters, possibly with partitions.

auditors visit a taxpayer's home and discover evidence that the office was also used as something else. For example, certain articles in the room—a sewing machine, a day bed, or children's toys—might be used to support the position that the office is actually a guestroom or a child's playroom.

The key is to demonstrate that the space was used exclusively on a regular basis; that means you have to show *continuing* use in your particular work—not just occasional or incidental use.

The Focal Point Test: Revising the Old Rules

A few years ago, the U.S. Supreme Court got involved in setting the rules of the game for the home office expenses deduction. At that time, small business owners were introduced to a new test that had to be satisfied to secure their deduction. The so-called "focal point test" tended not only to tighten the rules. It created a sense of confusion that led many to simply forget about writing off the business portion of their homes. Current law has relaxed some definitions, giving hope to some small business owners who work out of their homes. But you must understand the old rules as well as the new ones.

The focal point test suggested that your true place of business is at the point where goods and services are being rendered or delivered. Greater emphasis was given to the place where you see customers or patients than to the place where you tend to relatively less important details, such as billing or report writing.

The key determinant was not the amount of time spent at the place of business; rather it was the focal point—the place where the important part of the business transactions occur. This had become the key to securing the home office deduction.

For example, under the old rules, a doctor would have been denied the home office deduction if she spent the majority of her time visiting patients and consulting at various locations while spending only a day or two per week in the home office handling administrative duties.

Tax Law Update

However, under the current law, the definition of "principal place of business" has been relaxed to include a place of business in which the small business owner carries on administrative or management activities of his trade or business if there is no other fixed location available to conduct those duties. In fact, the law becomes even more lenient by stating that taxpayers who happen to perform administrative or management activities for their trade or business at places away from their home office will not necessarily be denied the home office deduction. In short, their home office could still be deemed to be their principal place of business.

Illustration 11.1

Diane is a self-employed costume jewelry retailer. She places orders from wholesalers and sells the jewelry at craft shows, on consignment, and through mail orders.

Diane spends about 15 hours per week at home placing orders, shipping, and keeping her books. She also spends 25 hours per week at craft shows and other marketing locations.

In this example, the IRS states that Diane is entitled to claim the home office deduction. Clearly, her home office was used "regularly and exclusively" as the only place for conducting administrative or management activities.

The message is clear. Many taxpayers have not tried to deduct their home office because of the Supreme Court's well-publicized position on the focal point test. The bottom line is that *the focal point test is not necessarily the only test*, particularly when it is unclear where the principal place of business is located.

PUTTING EXCLUSIVE BUSINESS USE RULE TO THE TEST

If you have ever gone through the exercise of calculating your home office expense, you may have been dismayed by the surprisingly small deduction as a result of your efforts. Those who clearly qualify for the home office deduction often limit themselves to the bare minimum to avoid the wrath of the IRS. Many feel that claiming more than 10 percent to 15 percent of the home is just asking for trouble.

The issue has been brought before the tax court, and from the court's ruling, it appears that no set norms for calculating the allocation of business use of your home exist, although you can attract an audit with an allocation that is too large. As explained in Illustration 11.2, the tax court had no problem allowing a major portion of a married couple's ranch-style house, which was dedicated exclusively to business use.

Illustration 11.2

Ron and Rose operate a home-based business printing legal documents in Columbus, Ohio. In their home office they keep various pieces of equipment, including machines needed to duplicate the documents, as well as computer systems for word processing and for reading materials.

The couple originally tried to deduct 94 percent of the home (nearly the entire house) for the years 1985 through 1987.

An IRS audit revealed 64 percent of the home should be allowed as a deduction.

After a follow-up with the tax court, it was decided that 78 percent of the total usable space was used exclusively for business and, thus, could be deducted.

Two observations in this decision highlighted in Illustration 11.2 should capture your attention as a small business owner. First, observe the importance of the calculation of floor space used for business. Second, look at the real meaning of the term *exclusive business use*.

CALCULATING THE FLOOR SPACE USED FOR BUSINESS

In Ron and Rose's case, the tax court set a precedent when it allowed an additional deduction for space in their house that the IRS ordinarily would consider as nonfunctional or having minimum usability. Here, the attic, which was used to store shipping and packing materials, was allowed—in spite of its sloping roof and awkward design.

DETERMINING EXCLUSIVE BUSINESS USE

The tax court also made another interesting concession when it allowed, as part of the home office allocation, the expenses attributable to the couple's garage. Although the garage housed two large printing presses and a paper cutter, the court observed that some nominal personal property items were also stored there. This usually gives the IRS enough ammunition to disallow the use of any room or area of one's home.

However, breaking with the traditional definition of exclusive business use, the tax court found that the IRS was oversensitive in its argument. The court felt that the lawnmower stored in the couple's garage was a matter too trivial to warrant disallowance of the deduction.

The lesson here is to be aware of the space you utilize for your home business operations. Look around your home office areas. Are there any personal items you should remove? Keep a keen eye for ways to increase the tax deductibility of your operation.

What to Expect When You Sell Your Home

Thanks to the revolutionary 1997 tax law change, taxpayers can now exclude up to $250,000 of gain on the sale of a personal residence. Married couples can exclude up to $500,000. In general, all you need to do to take advantage of the exclusion is to own and use the property as a "principal residence" for at least two of the five years before the sale. The two years do not even have to be consecutive. This provision opens up some wonderful planning opportunities for anyone who plans to sell his or her home some day.

However, to prevent taxpayers from having their cake and eating it too, the government decided that a certain amount of payback is due when a portion of the home was used for business. Small business owners should be aware of a tax trap when they sell a home for which they have claimed home office deductions. Assuming the home is sold at a gain, taxpayers must pay tax on the total amount of depreciation claimed after May 6, 1997. Although this may seem like bad news, this is actually a modest price to pay in view of the tax saving benefits previously obtained.

Illustration 11.3

Reggie had an office within his home for which he claimed depreciation deductions of $10,000 before May 6, 1997, and $3,000 after that date. The house was sold on June 1, 2003, generating a gain of $200,000.

Reggie can exclude $197,000 of the gain from taxes. He is only liable to report $3,000 of the gain on his 2003 tax return (the depreciation after the new transition date).

Good News When You Sell Your Home

In the past, there were lingering questions as to how the IRS might ultimately deal with the incredibly favorable tax treatment being handed out to those who sell homes that had been partially used as a business property. The idea that up to $500,000 in taxable gain could be excluded when mixed-use property was sold sounded too good to be true.

But now it's settled, thanks to an IRS regulation written in December 2002. Now, when a mixed-use, personal residence is sold at a profit, the only income that must be reported is that with regard to the depreciation claimed after May 6, 1997 (a comparatively small price to pay). In short, vast amounts of appreciated value in your property will be untouched by the IRS as long as you satisfy the two-out-of-five-years rule.

Put another way, you no longer need to worry about allocating the gain on sale between the residential and nonresidential portions of your property as long as they are within the same dwelling unit.

The only real trap comes if the home office is in a separate structure, such as a converted, detached garage. In the government's view, the home must be divided into two assets. The business portion is treated as the sale of a business asset rather than personal and therefore does not qualify for the personal residence gain exclusion. Calculations must be made to report the "taxable" gain on the business portion that was sold.

> What happens if your office is in a separate structure and you have to sell your personal residence at a loss? The very same rules that force you to recognize gain, described above, will then work to your tax advantage. Although no deduction is allowed for the sale of a personal asset (such as a primary residence) at a loss, business losses are fully deductible. In that case, you could at least recoup some of your loss through tax deductions for the business portion of your home.

K eep in mind you do not have to own your home to claim home office deductions. Assuming other guidelines are followed (such as the regular and exclusive use test), renters may deduct a portion of their housing expenses and not have to worry about potential gains when they move. For this reason, many tax professionals are more comfortable recommending the home office to those who rent rather than to those who own their homes.

Chapter Summary

Clearly, the increase in the number of home-based businesses over the last few years shows that this trend is here to stay. Individuals using their home offices either part-time or full-time must be wary of the tax implications.

As pointed out in this chapter, the current tax law focuses on the principal place of business (including administrative use) or a place to meet with clients in the normal course of business. If you intend on claiming a deduction for your home office, can you meet the requirements of either of these tests? Also, have you considered the long-term tax consequences—specifically the ramifications of the eventual sale of your home?

One thing is for certain, as more taxpayers claim this controversial deduction, there will be more IRS auditors looking for misuse or abuse. Your best plan is to remain informed of the latest tax law legislation.

12

Smart Retirement Planning and Tax Deferrals

ANY TECHNIQUE THAT ALLOWS A LEGAL DEFERMENT OF INCOME TAX LIABILITY will always be attractive to taxpayers. In an era of high tax rates, smart business owners are particularly interested in securing every possible tax-deferral measure.

New Law: 2001 Tax Act

The Economic Growth and Tax Relief Reconciliation Act of 2001 (2001 Tax Act) made sweeping changes in the area of retirement plans for the years 2002 and beyond. The annual limits on contributions to all types of plans were increased, along with other tax-favored incentives to encourage retirement savings. As a result, every small business owner should re-evaluate her or his retirement planning strategy. These changes will be explored in more detail throughout this chapter.

Employer Retirement Plans

Heading the list of legal tax-deferral schemes are the employer plans that provide retirement benefits for employees. At their best, these plans offer the luxury of an up-front tax deduction by the employer, while no taxable income needs to be reported by the affected employee. As income is generated from the invested funds in the plan, continued tax deferral allows for further, compounding tax advantages.

The real tax savings of a qualified retirement plan in action is shown in Illustration 12.1.

Illustration 12.1

Quill Corporation, owned by Dexter, Ellen, and Frances, approaches the end of its business year with a projected $15,000 profit.

The original plan was to pay Dexter, Ellen, and Frances, also the corporation's only employees, $5,000 each for the extra time and effort spent with the business that year.

Because they were all in the 33 percent tax bracket, Dexter, Ellen, and Frances arranged for the three $5,000 payments to go into a qualified retirement plan instead.

Quill Corporation is allowed a $15,000 up-front deduction.

Dexter, Ellen, and Frances are each spared from paying $1,650 on their share of bonuses ($5,000 multiplied by 33 percent).

In addition, the $15,000 invested by the plan will be allowed to compound, fully tax-deferred, during future years.

Interestingly, many small business owner-operators don't bother to take advantage of an employer-sponsored retirement plan because they are simply intimidated by its complexity. Further, many are not certain as to the *amount* of possible tax deferral that can be attained under today's complex rules. You may ask, "How much deferral makes sense at this time?"

A single chapter cannot begin to provide all the answers concerning this highly specialized and complex topic. However, you will at least be left informed as to the general choices of tax-favored plans that are now available under the current law. In addition, you should have a better idea as to which would meet your particular needs for tax saving retirement benefits.

The tax-favored retirement plan options for the small business owner are

◆ the Individual Retirement Account (IRA) and

◆ company-qualified plans.

Before you follow the traditional approach of deciphering each of the tax-favored retirement plans in their given order, first ask yourself the following two questions:

1. Which plan is the simplest and least cumbersome to operate in securing my retirement planning objectives?

2. Which will allow the most tax write-off without requiring an unnecessarily high cost of administration?

Then take a look at the plan alternatives in view of these underlying questions.

The Traditional IRA

Without question, the IRA is clearly the simplest and least expensive plan to set up and operate. Because of its simplicity and low costs, many small business owners choose the IRA because they don't want to be bothered with anything more complex. The problem, as you are probably well aware, is that the amount that can be socked away as a deductible contribution is quite limited.

TAX LAW UPDATE

For more than 20 years, annual contributions to an IRA were limited to $2,000 of your earnings, provided you have wages, salary, or self-employment. However, under the 2001 Tax Act, this contribution was raised to $3,000 beginning in 2002 and will eventually rise to $5,000 in 2008.

In addition, taxpayers who are at least age 50 by the year-end are entitled to special "catch-up" contributions of $500 for the years 2002 through 2005 and $1,000 for 2006 through 2008. Table 12-1 summarizes the new limits.

Spousal IRAs

Since 1997, a taxpayer's nonworking or low-earning spouse has been allowed an additional full contribution amount as long as their combined compensation is that much.

Tax Year	Annual Limit if Under Age 50	Annual Limit if Age 50 or More
2002	$3,000	$3,500
2003	$3,000	$3,500
2004	$3,000	$3,500
2005	$4,000	$4,500
2006	$4,000	$5,000
2007	$4,000	$5,000
2008	$5,000	$6,000

Table 12-1. **IRA limits**

Income Phase-Out Rules on Deductions

If you are an active participant in another employer retirement plan, that deduction is reduced under the income limitations shown in Table 12-2.

Taxable Years Beginning in	Phase-Out Range for Joint Returns	Phase-Out Range for Single Taxpayers
2002	$54,000–$64,000	$34,000–$44,000
2003	$60,000–$70,000	$40,000–$50,000
2004	$65,000–$75,000	$45,000–$55,000
2005	$70,000–$80,000	$50,000–$60,000
2006	$75,000–$85,000	$50,000–$60,000
2007 and thereafter	$80,00–$100,000	$50,000–$60,000

Figure 12-2. **Phase-Out rules**

An individual (including a nonworking spouse) is no longer considered an active participant in a retirement plan simply because his or her spouse is an active participant in the plan. However, when one spouse is an active participant, the nonactive spouse's ability to make a *deductible* contribution to his or her own IRA is phased out when the couple's combined AGI is between $150,000 and $160,000.

Tax Credit for Contributions After 2001

For taxpayers in the lower brackets, the deduction achieved by IRA contributions yields only a modest reduction in tax. Many small business owners decided their money would be better spent invested in the business, rather than an IRA that can't be touched until retirement— when they could very well be in a much higher tax bracket.

As a result, the new law encourages lower-income retirement savings with a credit for up to 50 percent of the first $2,000 contributed to IRAs for the years 2002 through 2006. This new credit is *in addition* to any deduction or exclusion that you otherwise get for your contributions.

The credit rate is determined by the taxpayer's adjusted income, as shown in Table 12-3.

Joint Filers	Heads of Households	All Others	Credit Rate
$0 - $30,000	$0 - $22,500	$0 - $15,000	50%
$30,001 - $32,500	$22,501 - $24,375	$15,001 - $16,250	20%
$32,501 - $50,000	$24,376 - $37,500	$16,251 - $25,000	10%
Over $50,000	Over $37,500	Over $25,000	0%

Table 12-3. Lower income credit rates

Besides the income limitations shown above, a few other restrictions apply. The credit is reduced by certain types of retirement plan distributions taken anytime during the last two years through the due date of the current year's return. Also, you must be over age 17 and cannot be a full-time student or claimed as a dependent on someone else's tax return. The credit also applies to contributions to Roth IRAs and "elective deferrals" to 401(k) plans and SIMPLE plans, which will be discussed later in this chapter.

With this new credit, lower-income taxpayers now have a much greater incentive to save for retirement, as explained in Illustration 12.2.

Illustration 12.2
Ralph, a married man, owns a small construction company with three employees.

The company generated a rather meager profit during the current year. His wife participates in a qualified retirement plan.

With a modest AGI of $24,000, Ralph finds himself in the 15 percent tax bracket for 2003.

Although short on cash, he begins an IRA for himself at no administrative cost. To this account he contributes the maximum $3,000.

Ralph saves a whopping $1,450 in taxes that year: $3,000 multiplied by 15 percent ($450) plus 50 percent of $2,000 ($1,000). He also gets to participate in an investment program that will accumulate tax-free dollars compounded annually for future years.

In essence, Ralph just got the government to fund nearly half of his current year retirement contributions!

Special Note: For all tax-favored retirement plans, the participant is not permitted to take distributions from the retirement account until age 59½—except in unique circumstances—without incurring a penalty.

Q. Where can your IRA contributions be invested?
A. The assets of an IRA account must be invested in a trustee or custodial account with a bank, savings and loan association, credit union, brokerage firm, or other qualified person operating as trustee or custodian. However, you can stay in charge and direct the investment plan yourself as long as you put your money into vehicles like certificates of deposit, stocks, bonds, mutual funds, annuity contracts, and a few other specified areas. To establish an IRA account, refer to IRS Form 5305.

The Roth IRA

When Congress passed the Taxpayer Relief Act of 1997, it created an entirely new dimension in the art of retirement planning. Although the decision to establish a Roth IRA is not one for business owners specifically, its widespread popularity makes it important for the purpose of tax saving. In short, it is available to all taxpayers who have earned income as long as certain general income limitations are met.

Although contributions to a Roth IRA are nondeductible, the real value is that a participant can put away money each year and watch it grow tax-free until it comes time to pull out distributions. The key benefit, however, is that the distributions can be taken out tax free after five years as long as that individual has reached age 59½.

Clearly, the ability to receive tax-free distributions to supplement your retirement income stream makes for an attractive retirement planning alternative—one that needs to be explored by all taxpayers.

Q. How much can I contribute to a Roth IRA?

A. You can contribute up to the annual IRA limit (generally $3,000 for 2002 through 2004), provided you have earned that much in compensation. However, there are limitations for higher earners. Your ability to contribute to a Roth is phased out if you are single when your adjusted gross income is between $95,000 and $110,000. If you are married, the threshold is between $150,000 and $160,000.

Taxpayers may split the maximum annual IRA contribution limit between traditional and Roth IRAs. In short, it is available to all taxpayers who have earned income as long as certain general income limitations are met.

THE ROTH IRA ROLLOVER QUESTION

Perhaps the most-asked question about the popular Roth IRA is whether or not an individual should roll over his or her traditional IRA into a Roth plan to secure a tax-free income stream. This can be an extremely important question for those who are looking to enhance their planned cash flow at retirement with an attractive tax-free income stream.

In very general terms, all that you need to do is to roll over the IRA funds into the Roth plan within 60 days after receipt and to pay the tax on the distribution at that time. If you happen to be under age 59½, you will not be subject to the usual 10 percent penalty tax that is usually applied, as long as you meet a five-year holding period before taking any distributions.

Special Note: The qualified rollover cannot be made if your adjusted gross income is more than $100,000 or if you are married and filing a separate return and lived with your spouse during the year.

If you have a traditional IRA, carefully consider the possibility of rolling over your tax-deferred investment into a Roth plan. Although there may be something of a price to pay in terms of an initial tax cost, the long-range benefits may outweigh that cost in the long run. Also, if you have made nondeductible contributions to your traditional IRA, you will not be taxed on those particular contributions.

IRA Summary

For taxpayers with limited funds, the IRA is still a sound choice for a basic retirement plan. Those with lower incomes will particularly benefit from the new credit on contributions. IRAs also function well as a supplementary plan for more affluent taxpayers. Recent changes in the tax law increase contribution limits from the historical $2,000 per year to $3,000, and over time, this limit will increase to $5,000. The new law also provides for additional contributions of up to $500 per year for those who are at least 50 by year-end.

If eligible, taxpayers should carefully consider a Roth IRA over the traditional IRA, including conversions of low-balance traditional accounts to a Roth. While current contributions to a Roth IRA are non-deductible, retirement funds can be completely tax free down the road.

While simple and inexpensive to administer, IRAs still provide only a limited opportunity to defer taxes and accumulate funds for retirement. Employers may "sponsor" an IRA, and therefore coordinate contributions with payroll deductions, but both Roth and traditional IRAs are personal plans, as opposed to retirement plans of your business. The successful small business owner quickly "outgrows" personal IRAs and graduates to more complex plans that provide greater tax-saving opportunities.

Company Qualified Plans

If you have an ownership interest in a small business corporation and are concerned about the increasing tax bill on your profits, chances are you need to look closely at a *company qualified retirement plan*. Such plans often provide substantial tax write-offs up front. In addition, there are long-range benefits as your investment dollars compound and grow unfettered by current taxes. Before you participate, have an experienced pension consultant explain all the related costs and obligations that are part of the program. Also, remain aware that there are strict antidiscrimination rules, so that excessive retirement benefits cannot be allocated to owners and key employees in an unfair manner.

Consider Ralph from Illustration 12.2, who, after a point in time, witnesses some reasonable growth and development in the closely held corporation he operates. Assume that with his steadily increasing salary he is now well beyond the IRA stage. Illustration 12.3 shows what steps he might take.

Illustration 12.3

Ralph's corporation, during the last month of a particular fiscal year, projects a $20,000 profit. Ralph, in the 28 percent tax bracket that year, sees no economic merit to adding another $20,000 to his salary via his W-2.

He decides to set up a qualified retirement plan. Although his other two employees will be entitled to a small portion, $15,000 goes to Ralph's retirement account based on the plan.

The corporation can deduct the $20,000 contribution, leaving no corporate tax liability. Ralph pays no tax on the contribution. Further, he has $15,000 working for him tax free in his retirement plan account.

How are small business owners like Ralph supposed to know what kind of company qualified retirement plan is best for their purposes?

If you are a small corporate owner like Ralph, you need to look at all your retirement planning options before you start taking profits and paying excessive taxes on such. Before you start spending money on professional advisors and "pension experts," familiarize yourself with some of the general planning alternatives so you know which questions to ask.

In Ralph's case (as outlined in Illustration 12.3), before he "socked away" a hefty $15,000 he first had to contemplate some pervasive, long-range issues before he decided what kind of company qualified plan would be best for him. He had to consider that whichever plan he chose, there would be strict antidiscrimination rules to follow.

This meant he would have to evaluate the amount that would also have to be put in the plan for his other two employees each year. Even though he would probably continue to attain the lion's share of the benefits, an evaluation of the overall out-of-pocket costs must be made before deciding the best route.

If you decide that a qualified plan, with employees included, is a worthwhile endeavor, then ask yourself the following two questions:

1. Would I be better off with a plan that requires the company to contribute a certain percentage of employee's salaries every year or should I gear it to the profits of the company?

2. What is the maximum tax-free amount that can be legally "socked away" in the plan?

With these questions in mind, you will better appreciate the pros and cons of the general plan alternatives available with a company retirement plan.

Choosing the Right Company Plan

As a small business owner, you are faced with a multitude of choices in designing your company's retirement plan. Your general options are among several varieties of defined contribution plans, defined benefit plans, and simplified employee pensions (also known as SEPs or SEP-IRAs). Each type of plan is briefly introduced below and discussed in further detail later in the chapter. The charts at the end of this chapter compare features of each type of plan.

With a defined contribution type of retirement plan, an employer (and/or employee) makes a specific contribution into the plan on behalf of qualified employees, with no guarantees as to how much retirement income will be available to the individual. Common examples of defined contribution plans include money purchase pension plans, profit-sharing plans, 401(k) plans, and SIMPLE plans.

A defined benefit plan provides participants with a targeted monthly benefit at retirement and potentially allows the largest annual contributions on behalf of the owners. However, these types of plans are among the most expensive to set up and administer.

Finally, simplified employee pensions (SEPs) allow employers to make discretionary annual contributions based on compensation. Unlike other types of plans, which make contributions to a trust, employers can adopt a SEP agreement and make annual contributions directly to an account or annuity set up for each eligible employee. This type of arrangement greatly reduces both the employer's administrative burden and annual report obligations.

WHAT IF I'M SELF-EMPLOYED?

An individual starting out in business should be aware that the tax-saving benefits of retirement plans are available to self-employed individuals as well as owner-employees of corporations. Further, the qualification rules for self-employed plans are, in many regards, no different than those of corporate plans. For retirement plan purposes, the self-employed person is treated as both employer and employee. Even if you are self-employed and have no other employees, you can still qualify for these tax-saving benefits, as long as you have earned income during the taxable year.

"Earned income" refers to earnings with respect to a business in which personal services are a material factor. Self-employed individuals include lawyers, accountants, doctors, architects, and all types of consultants. It may also include those who operate a business such as real estate, home repair, a bakery, a gift shop, or independent sales.

As you will see, the contribution limits for many types of retirement plans are keyed to the individual's "compensation." For unincorporated businesses, the owner's compensation is the "net business profits." (For this purpose, net business profit is the business profit less one-half of the individual's self-employment tax).

REDUCED CONTRIBUTION RATE FOR SELF-EMPLOYED OWNERS

The actual amount of deductible contributions that you, the self-employed owner, can make on your own behalf is based on a special IRS formula. (Self-employed owners include sole proprietors, partners, and LLC members.)

Table 12-4 converts the plan's contribution rate to the rate owners can contribute for themselves.

Illustration 12.4

Reginald, a self-employed musician with no employees, checked over his records at the end of 2003 and learned that he had generated a net profit (after subtracting one-half self-employment tax) of $40,000 for the year.

Expecting that the profit from his business would be taxed at an uncomfortably high tax rate, Reginald quickly learned that (starting in 2002) the maximum contribution rate for SEP-IRAs had increased to 25 percent of compensation.

If the plan's contribution rate is (shown as percent)	Then your contribution rate is (shown as decimal)
1	.009901
2	.019608
3	.029126
4	.038462
5	.047619
6	.056604
7	.065421
8	.074074
9	.082569
10	.090909
11	.099099
12	.107143
13	.115044
14	.122807
15*	.130435
16	.137931
17	.145299
18	.152542
19	.159664
20	.166667
21	.173554
22	.180328
23	.186992
24	.193548
25 (maximum)	.200000

Table 12-4. **Reduced contribution rate for self-employed owners**

*The maximum contribution rate for profit-sharing plans and SEPs was 15 percent prior to 2002. For 2002 and beyond, that limit has been increased to 25 percent.

> To maximize his tax savings, he opted to set up a SEP-IRA plan with his broker, contribute and deduct the maximum amount allowable, and let it grow—tax-deferred—for his retirement.
>
> However, because Reginald is self-employed, the IRS makes him subtract the contribution itself from his net profits **before** applying the rate. To avoid a lot of complicated math, Reginald simply referred to the conversion table and saw that the plan's maximum contribution rate of 25 percent resulted in a 20 percent contribution for him.
>
> Reginald's maximum contribution amount for 2003 was therefore $8,000 ($40,000 x 20 percent) per the IRS conversion table.

Special Note: You may have heard about "Keogh" or "HR 10" plans for self-employed persons. Many years ago, unincorporated businesses could not establish the same types of retirement plans as corporations. Congress passed a special law (HR 10) to change this, and a key legislator was Senator Keogh. Thereafter, a "Keogh" or "HR 10" plan is simply a qualified plan typically set up by sole proprietors, LLCs and partnerships. The plans themselves may be defined contribution plans (either money purchase pension or profit sharing) or defined benefit plans. Other types of plans discussed, such as a SEP, 401(k), and the SIMPLE plans are also available to an unincorporated business but are not considered "Keoghs."

Key Observation: While a partnership or LLC (acting as a company) can establish a qualified plan, the individual members or partners themselves cannot, even though they otherwise have self-employment income. These rules are similar to those of a corporation and its employees. In other words, the company must set up the plan, not the individual.

The Defined Contribution Plans

Defined contribution plans consist of the four following basic types:

1. Money purchase pension plans
2. Profit sharing plans
3. 401(k) plans

4. SIMPLE plans

MONEY PURCHASE PENSION PLANS

With the money purchase pension plan, an employer makes an agreement promising to make a specific contribution into a retirement plan on behalf of the qualified employees. The contribution is usually an expressed percentage of the employee's compensation and is not based on profits. Thus, you need to be careful when you set these percentage requirements because you may be required to make retirement contributions in amounts that may be difficult to come up with during times of faltering cash flow and/or profits.

What Is the Maximum Contribution? The current maximum amount that can be contributed to an employee's account is 25 percent of the employee's compensation up to $200,000, subject to an overall limit of $40,000. The amount of compensation considered and the overall limit are set by the IRS and periodically adjusted.

For the unincorporated owner, the maximum contribution percentage drops to 20 percent and is applied to business profits less than one-half of self-employment tax. The $200,000 and $40,000 limits also apply to the self-employed.

Illustration 12.5

Jeff is an employee and the sole owner of Crinkle Corporation. He has one other employee, Fred.

Anticipating a $31,000 profit in the current year, Jeff sets up a money purchase pension plan. He elects to use the maximum contribution percentage of 25 percent.

With Jeff drawing a salary of $100,000 and Fred drawing $24,000, the corporation gets the maximum tax advantage.

The allowed contribution for Jeff is $25,000, or $100,000 multiplied by 25 percent. For Fred it's $6,000, or $24,000 multiplied by 25 percent. So with a total contribution of $31,000, Jeff has managed to eliminate any corporate tax liability for the year.

THE PROFIT-SHARING PLAN

The comforting advantage of the profit-sharing plan is that, for the most part, it provides you as the employer with a totally discretionary contribution formula. In other words, if you don't want to be obligated to make contributions each year, set up a profit-sharing plan that essentially states: *No profit, no contributions to the plan.*

> **Special Note:** Although an employer is not required to contribute any particular percentage of profits, the profit-sharing plan must have a written formula for allocating the profits consistently among the participants.

What Is the Maximum Contribution? Although limited in the past to 15 percent of compensation, since 2002, annual contribution limits for profit-sharing plans are the same as for the money purchase plans discussed earlier.

Therefore, contributions for employees are based on the first $200,000 of compensation, and the contribution percentage can be as high as 25 percent. Contributions for the *unincorporated* business owner are slightly less than for employees and max out at 20 percent of the first $200,000 of net profits less one-half of self-employment tax. All contributions on behalf of an individual are subject to an overall limit of $40,000 per person. The current $200,000 and $40,000 limits are as of 2002 and will most likely be adjusted in future years.

Consider the circumstances of Tanya (Illustration 12.6), the owner of a small consulting corporation with three people on the payroll, including her. Tanya anticipates some healthy profits over the next few years, but she has some long-range concerns about the company's continuing profitability. She decides that the best and most conservative retirement plan to choose from under the circumstances is a profit-sharing plan. For peace of mind, Tanya takes the position that "no profit, no obligation to make retirement contributions" is the best policy.

> **Illustration 12.6**
> Tanya anticipates a $20,000 corporate profit for the current year; she does not favor paying taxes on such.
> Tanya sets up a profit-sharing plan that calls for a contribution of 10 percent of each employee's salary for the year, including her own.

> **Key Observation:** As an employer, you may have one other option available with profit-sharing plans. You may elect to make a plan contribution

> Although she could contribute as much as 25 percent for the current year, the 10 percent contribution to the retirement plan is just enough to bring the corporate profits down to zero.
>
> Instead of paying corporate taxes on $20,000 that year, Tanya pays nothing.
>
> Tanya attains the conservative goal of her plan. A reasonable retirement plan is in place, and she is not saddled with future obligations when no profit or cash is available.

in a given year even though the corporation does **not** make a profit. This is a good idea if it makes sense to tie up cash dollars to get some long-range, tax-deferred benefits for the earnings on your investment.

Key Observation: Before 2002, annual contributions to a profit-sharing plan (and SEPs) were generally limited to 15 percent of compensation, while money purchase pension plan contributions could be based on up to 25 percent of individual earnings. Therefore, in order to maximize **available** contributions while minimizing **required** contributions, businesses would often set up two types of plans: a 15 percent discretionary profit-sharing plan (or SEP), plus a 10 percent mandatory money purchase pension plan. However, under recent tax law changes, profit-sharing plans and SEP's can now contribute just as much annually as a money purchase plan. As a result, **few informed business owners are choosing to establish money purchase plans now.**

401(k) Plans: A Rebirth

At its core, the 401(k) plan is a form of a salary reduction arrangement where employees (including owners) have the option to forgo a certain amount of income and have it put into a retirement plan instead. Employees can defer a por-

> If you already have a money purchase plan, consider replacing it with a less rigid profit-sharing plan or SEP for tax years after 2002.

tion of their *W-2* income, and unincorporated business owners can contribute part of the before-tax net earnings from the business. While still subject to FICA, the "elective deferral" amount escapes current federal income tax.

The amount each person can defer per year is limited, as follows, depending on whether or not the participant is over age 50 by year-end:

Tax Year	Annual Limit if Under Age 50	Annual Limit if Age 50 or More
2002	$11,000	$12,000
2003	$12,000	$14,000
2004	$13,000	$16,000
2005	$14,000	$18,000
2006	$15,000	$20,000

Table 12-5. Limitations on salary deferrals

The 401(k) plan is generally tied to a profit-sharing plan, which can now provide employer contributions of up to 25 percent compensation. In the past, any profit-sharing contributions had to be reduced by the employee's elective deferral. However, for tax years after 2001, the two contributions are made independently, subject to the annual overall limit ($40,000 for 2002).

Although this may not sound like a big change, the impact is tremendous. By raising the annual contribution percentage of a profit-sharing plan from 15 percent to 25 percent, *and* decoupling the elective deferrals from the employer's contribution, the 2001 Tax Act transforms the once humble 401(k) plan into a fierce contender as the retirement plan of choice for a small business. At all income levels, the 401(k) now provides the maximum retirement plan contributions for business owners, with the possible exception of a defined benefit plan.

An added advantage is the flexibility provided to both the owner and the ordinary employee. For the profit-sharing plan contribution, the owner has the discretion to set funding percentages each year. Likewise, the "elective deferral" portion is controlled by the individual, who can adjust contributions on at least an annual basis (more often, if the plan allows).

Planning Idea: If you already have a profit-sharing plan, consider adding a 401(k) plan as a supplement. Employee deferrals, if any, are set and funded by the employee. Meanwhile, you could greatly enhance your ability to fund your own retirement in years when the business income alone does not put your profit-sharing contribution at the annual maximum.

Five Special Requirements to Qualify for a 401(k) Plan

1. The employee-participant must be given the option of having the employer give the employee cash or make the contribution to the plan.
2. The plan must prohibit certain early distributions to the employee.
3. The employee-participants must have certain vested rights to the value of their account at all times.
4. The plan cannot require, as a condition of participation in the plan, that an employee complete more than one year of service with the employer.
5. It cannot make conditions to get benefits under the 401(k) plan that are based on the employee's elective contributions.

The SIMPLE IRA

Portions of the following article, titled "Finally, A Retirement Plan Small Businesses Can Afford," by Jim Vonachen are reprinted with permission from The McGraw-Hill Companies, Inc.

> When you're reading a book on taxes, it's good to know there's something in the IRS code that's cause for celebration. It's the new, congressionally mandated SIMPLE-IRA plans. This fresh twist on the individual retirement account lets more small business owners save for their own—and their employees'—retirement while greatly increasing regulatory burdens that may have discouraged them in the past.
>
> Congress, of course, is gaga over acronyms, and it dubbed the Savings Incentive Matching Plan for Employees (SIMPLE) to signify the streamlined paperwork requirements for small businesses setting up these plans.
>
> While the SIMPLE regulations are easier and cheaper to digest than the previous rules, they are, alas, a product of Congress and the IRS, which means they're not that simple. To make the best use of them, it's helpful to trace their family tree.

By now you've probably discovered the first rule of small business retirement planning. It's hard to do. That's mainly because of expense but also because of the IRS rules that govern so-called qualified plans like 401(k)s. (The term "qualified" simply means a plan conforms to specified limits on the amount the owner of a business can contribute in comparison to his lowest-paid employee.)

Qualified plans, however, are by far the most lucrative way to save funds for retirement. The employer gets a tax deduction for money going into the plan, and both employees and employer-owners get to watch their contributions grow tax free.

Aside from finding money to fund a qualified plan, small businesses have had to cope with:

◆ *The cost of starting a plan, normally $1,000 to $2,000. Ongoing administrative changes can easily run more than $75 per employee, per year, since small employers typically hire an outside service to keep track of the plan.*

◆ *The additional cost and complexity of meeting the IRS's discrimination rules that determine if top management's saving options are unfairly generous compared to other employees'. The IRS-required start-up documentation often totals 50 to 75 pages.*

◆ *The cost of educating employees about the savings plans as well as the cost of completing annual IRS and Labor Department reports. Penalties are levied on companies that file improperly.*

Of course, larger employers can more easily absorb the costs and risks of these qualified plans. For them, annual administrative expenses can run as low as $25 per participant, which is three to four times less than the typical cost to small companies.

The bottom line: For small-business owners to run a qualified plan they not only have to spend thousands of start-up dollars but they also must invest substantial time and money in record-keeping, employee education, and government compliance. And this doesn't even include the actual cash contributions to employees' plans. In all, qualified plans demand a level of commitment few small businesses are capable of meeting.

In the past, an alternative to qualified plans was the Simplified Employee Pension (SEP) and a more recent variation—the SEP coupled with a Salary Reduction feature (SAR-SEP).

Despite its complexities, the SAR-SEP was still much less complex than a 401(k). But as part of new tax laws, SAR-SEPs were discontinued as of December 31, 1996. Congress intends for the SIMPLE to replace the SAR-SEP, although existing SAR-SEPs can continue under the prior rules.

Given this background—the complicated compliance rules and the fact that SEP and SAR-SEP plans were not attracting the participants Congress had hoped for—the lawmakers authorized the SIMPLE-IRA, a new form of the Individual Retirement Account.

Do not confuse the SIMPLE-IRA with the SIMPLE 401(k). Although they are similar in many respects, the SIMPLE 401(k) is not nearly as advantageous to the employer as the SIMPLE-IRA. Since the SIMPLE 401(k) must meet many of the same requirements as a traditional "qualified" 401(k), the cost is substantially higher to business owners.

The first rule of the SIMPLE-IRA is to forget all of the rules for qualified and SEP plans. Qualified plans and SEPs are designed for the primary benefit and protection of employees. SIMPLE-IRA plans are designed for their benefit, too, but offer employers much more discretion. Congress shifted the emphasis because it found small businesses were wary of the other plans' red tape. That virtually paralyzed their retirement offerings. Now, the qualified plans' discrimination tests are gone.

The SIMPLE-IRA allows for employees (as well as the business owner) to place up to $7,000 of salary into an IRA account. Employees contribute pretax dollars, which lowers their taxable income, and thus their income tax, just as would happen with a 401(k). Of course, once the funds are deposited into an IRA account, they are governed by most standing IRA rules!

Employers can save money for their own retirement plan regardless of whether employees do so or not. The maximum total amount per year is $13,000 — $7,000 of salary deferral plus a 3 percent match on a salary of $200,000 or more.

The 2001 Tax Act increased the amount of annual salary deferrals for SIMPLE-IRAs as explained below.

Technical Requirements for the SIMPLE-IRA

Employees must be given 60 days each year to decide whether or not

Tax Year	Annual Salary Deferral Limit if Under Age 50	Annual Salary Deferral Limit if Age 50 or More
2002	$7,000	$7,500
2003	$8,000	$9,000
2004	$9,000	$10,500
2005	$10,000	$12,000
2006	$10,000	$12,500

Table 12-6. **Annual salary deferrals for SIMPLE-IRAs**

to participate in the plan. And to be an eligible sponsor of a SIMPLE-IRA, an employer must have had 100 or fewer employees receiving compensation of $5,000 or more each the preceding tax year. Once an employer has established a valid SIMPLE plan, he or she may generally be able to continue on the program for two more years even if the number of employees exceeds 100.

There is no long-term fixed commitment on the behalf of an employer. Once started, the law only requires that the plan run for the entire calendar year, although it can be terminated the next year. Further, a plan document is required—the six-page IRS Form 5305 SIMPLE or a commercial provider's prototype document. This once-a-year filing is the only necessary IRS form.

The SIMPLE-IRA must be offered to all employees who have received at least $5,000 of compensation in at least two prior years and those who expect to receive at least $5,000 of compensation in the current year. Note, these are minimum requirements. An employer can choose to lower cutoffs as well. As an employer, you can choose to exclude union employees, certain airline pilots, and nonresident aliens who receive non-U.S. source income from the plan and you cannot maintain any other active qualified plan or SEP plan while the SIMPLE-IRA is in existence. Keep in mind: employee salary deferrals are subject to Social Security and federal unemployment taxes.

Once an employee has decided to participate in the SIMPLE-IRA, he or she can end participation at any time, though once an employee has dropped out of the plan, that individual cannot re-enter until the start of the next year. Also, an employer has the option of allowing participants to modify their salary deferrals during the course of the year. Thus, the employer could present the employee-participants with the option of either terminating all participation in the plan or requiring employees to maintain a designated level of contributions.

This flexibility only increases the plan's attractiveness to a small-business owner. Its main attraction, of course, is savings in administrative costs. Since start-up fees are minimal and employees' own contributions fund most of the savings, an employer can offer a means of retirement savings without going broke. Part of the plan, however, does require employers to contribute a small percentage to the employees' savings. The contribution can be either in the form of an employer match or an across-the-board contribution.

The SIMPLE-IRA can be a very effective retirement vehicle for your small business. The pervasive marketing of plans by financial service companies—which will set up plans for you—makes them sound like the solution for every small business. That may not always be the case, but they do provide significant benefits to employers who want to reduce the cost of retirement programs while at the same time funding their own retirement.

Simplified Employee Pension Plan (SEP)

Suppose you like the low administration burden of a SIMPLE- IRA but not the low contribution limits? In that case, the simplified employee pension may be the answer you're looking for.

A SEP plan set up by small business owners allows contributions to an IRA account set up by or for their employees. The key, however, is that the amount contributed can go well beyond the usual restrictive IRA limitations and the increased limits of a SIMPLE-IRA.

What It Takes to Be Eligible

One nice feature about the SEP retirement plan it that it may be entirely discretionary each year. If you, the small business owner, don't have the funds in any one year, you simply don't have to make any contributions to the plan. When you *do* make a contribution, you must cover anybody who

- is over 21 years old;

- earns more than $450 during the year (based on a 2002 figure);

- has worked for you at *any* time during at least three of the past five years.

The SEP retirement plan is thought of as a simple, convenient arrangement that can be used by almost any small business, provided there is no discrimination in favor of the owner-employees or those who are highly compensated. Thus, a corporation, a partnership, LLC, or a sole proprietorship can qualify.

Q. How much can be contributed to and deducted from a SEP plan?
A. Contribution limits for SEPs are the same as those for the money purchase pension and profit-sharing plans, discussed earlier.

If you plan to implement a SEP plan, remember that you are getting into a wholly employer-funded arrangement. If you have the available cash and wish to contribute something to a retirement plan for yourself and your employees across the board, then this plan is for you.

Illustration 12.7

Marco, the owner of Zenith Corporation, anticipates a $30,000 profit for the current year.

Marco draws $60,000 in salary, while his one employee, Marie, draws $50,000.

Mindful of the extra cash reserves on hand, Zenith sets up a SEP-IRA account. The maximum is contributed to a SEP-IRA account that Marco opens for himself and Marie.

Zenith gets a deductible contribution of $27,000, with a flat 25 percent discretionary payment. A total of $15,000 goes to Marco's account ($60,000 multiplied by 25 percent) and $12,500 to Marie's account ($50,000 multiplied by 25 percent).

The Defined Benefit Plan: The Ultimate In Tax-Favored Retirement Benefits

Unlike other qualified retirement plans whereby contributions are usually based on a flat percentage of employee's salaries, the *defined benefit* arrangement allows for some major exceptions to the deduction limits. The key is that this special plan permits deductions for the required amount to fund the retirement plan so that it meets your planning objective. Your objective, of course, is to secure a targeted amount of retirement benefits that you need to be comfortable when you reach the "magic" age of 59½, or a later retirement age if you so choose.

> **Illustration 12.8**
>
> Marla owns 100 percent of Presley Corporation, which is anticipated to generate about $60,000 in income for the current year. During the year, she earns $45,000 in salary, while her other three employees earn $200,000 each.
>
> Marla, the only employee close to retirement, sets up a defined benefit plan for the current year. This type of plan calls for a substantial contribution on her behalf to meet this targeted retirement objective.
>
> With help from a pension consultant, it is theoretically possible that a $60,000 deductible contribution can be made to the defined benefit plan—with $50,000 (an amount more than her salary) going to Marla's account and the balance going to the employees.
>
> The deduction would, of course, eliminate any tax liability.

Key Observation: Although the defined benefit plan is usually designed to allow a larger contribution benefit for the owner-participant, its advantages are not as significant as with corporate defined benefit arrangements. Generally, when such plans are run through self-employed Keogh plans, the most that can be contributed for the owner is limited to the self-employed individual's net income for the year. You will recall that with corporate plans, the contributions can in some cases go well beyond the owner-participant's compensation.

Key Observation: Actuarial assumptions and computations are required to figure the annual contributions to a defined benefit plan; therefore, you will need continuing professional help with this type of plan. If significant administrative costs are something you want to avoid, then the defined benefit plan is not for you.

Additional Changes from the 2001 Tax Act

TAX CREDIT FOR PLAN START-UP COSTS

By some estimates, less than 30 percent of the millions of people working for small businesses in America have the opportunity to participate in a retirement plan. One reason small business owners often give for not starting a retirement plan is the administrative cost associated with getting a plan established.

In an effort to encourage small businesses with employees to make the leap into retirement plans, the 2001 Tax Act creates a credit for employers that start a new retirement plan after 2001. The credit equals 50 percent of the first $1,000 spent to set up, administer, and educate employees about the plan, and is available for each of the first three years of the plan.

In order to receive the credit, you must meet the following criteria:

◆ The business cannot have employed, in the preceding year, more than 100 employees receiving compensation of more than $5,000.

◆ At least one participant must be a non-highly compensated employee.

◆ The employees generally cannot be substantially the same employees covered by another retirement plan of your business (or a business you control) in the past three years.

PLAN LOANS

The 2001 Tax Act also made changes to the rules on retirement plan loans. In the past, ordinary employees could take a loan from certain qualified retirement plans (generally money purchase pensions, profit-sharing, and 401(k) plans), a benefit that was denied to the business's owners. However, for tax years beginning after 2001, owners receive the same treatment as other employees. Keep in mind, all plan loans are restricted in the amount that can be loaned, and repayment terms are subject to IRS guidelines.

Chapter Summary

It can be argued that the most effective way to secure relief from your oppressive income tax liability is to contribute to a tax-deductible retirement plan. In addition to the immediate tax savings, the contributor secures the following benefits:

- ◆ The long-term benefit of having his or her investment compound and grow tax free all the way to retirement

- ◆ A program to set the stage for continuing and systematic savings plans that she or he would ordinarily not adhere to

Fortunately, for the small business owner, a number of options may be considered to gain the best advantage. The options range from the most basic IRA to the most complex pension or profit-sharing arrangement. Every small business owner should take a look at each of these options before deciding which makes the best sense in terms of the lowest cost to set up, the least amount of effort to operate, and the maximum tax savings.

	Traditional or Roth IRA	Money Purchase Pension	Profit Sharing	401(k)	SIMPLE	SEP	Defined Benefit
Who makes contribution?	Individual	Company	Company	Both	Both	Company	Company
Are employer contributions mandatory?	N/A	Yes	No	No	Yes	No	Yes
Contribution limits if owner of unincorporated business	Up to $3,000 ($3,500 if age 50+)	Up to 20% of first $200,000 in net business income; overall limit of $40,000	Up to 20% of first $200,000 in net business income; overall limit of $40,000	Employee may defer up to $11,000 ($12,000 if age 50+) plus employer profit sharing contribution. Overall limit is $40,000 ($41,000 if at least age 50)	Employee may defer up to $7,000 ($7,500 if age 50+). Mandatory employer contributions are either matching contributions up to 3% of compensation or flat 2% of compensation.	Up to 20% of first $200,000 in net business income; overall limit of $40,000	Determined by actuarial assumptions and computations
Contribution limits if an employee (including corporate owners)	Same	Up to 25% of the first $200,000 in compensation; overall limit of $40,000	Up to 25% of the first $200,000 in compensation; overall limit of $40,000	Employee may add profit sharing employer contributions. Overall limit is $40,000 ($41,000 if at least age 50)		Up to 25% of the first $200,000 in compensation; overall limit of $40,000	Same
Administrative burden	Lowest	High	High	High	Low	Low	Highest

Table 12-7. 2002 retirement plan comparison chart

The following charts compare contribution limits at various income levels for the most popular retirement plan options. The amounts shown combine potential elective deferrals with employer contributions, to let you see the total amount you as an owner can put away for your retirement.

Self-Employment Income[1]	$10,000	$50,000	$100,000	$200,000
SEP-IRA	$2,000	$10,000	$20,000	$30,000
Profit Sharing	$2,000	$10,000	$20,000	$30,000
Money Purchase Pension	$2,000	$10,000	$20,000	$30,000
Simple IRA •Under age 50 •Age 50+	$7,300 $7,800	$8,500 $9,000	$10,000 $10,500	$11,500 $12,000
401(k) •Under age 50 •Age 50+	$10,000 $10,000	$21,000 $22,000	$31,000 $32,000	$40,000 $41,000

1. Net business profit minus one-half of self-employment tax.

Table 12-8. **Maximum deductible contributions for unincorporated businesses**

W-2 Income	$10,000	$50,000	$100,000	$200,000
SEP-IRA	$2,500	$12,500	$25,000	$37,500
Profit Sharing	$2,500	$12,500	$25,000	$37,500
Money Purchase Pension	$2,500	$12,500	$25,000	$37,500
Simple IRA •Under age 50 •Age 50+	$7,300 $7,800	$8,500 $9,000	$10,000 $10,500	$11,500 $12,000
401(k) •Under age 50 •Age 50+	$10,000 $10,000	$23,500 $24,500	$36,000 $37,000	$40,000 $41,000

Table 12-9. **Maximum deductible contributions for incorporated businesses**

13

Understanding Family Planning Tax Strategies

WHEN YOU SHIFT INCOME AND ASSETS TO OTHER FAMILY MEMBERS, YOU will encounter a number of income tax savings advantages in addition to the potential estate planning advantages. Tax savings are clearly available to small business owners who shift business ownership and business income from their higher tax bracket to the lower brackets of other family members. In previous years, taxpayers didn't use this tax saving tactic for three reasons.

1. There weren't enough tax savings to make it worth the effort. The difference between the parents' and the children's tax rates was usually too small to generate an overall significant tax savings.

2. Too many feared loss of control when turning over the ownership of assets to younger, less experienced family members.

3. Many feared the IRS's repercussions for maneuvering with such an aggressive tax-shelter procedure.

Each one of these is a legitimate issue. However, the facts are often distorted and can sometimes be considered downright myths.

Can You Save Enough Taxes by Splitting Income?

Whether you operate as a corporation, a partnership, an LLC, or a sole proprietorship, the final measure of savings will directly depend on your current *individual* tax rate. (To better understand your individual rate, refer back to Chapter 1.)

All business owners, at one time or another, have to account for business profits on their personal tax returns. If enough disparity exists between the income and tax bracket of one family member and that of another, there could be an opportunity to save significant tax dollars. The only way to be certain of this is to check your tax brackets and run a computation. *Remember, the strategy does not work between husband and wife.*

Illustration 13.1

Small business owner Eileen has been relegated to the 28 percent tax bracket for 2003.

She determines that her 19-year-old son, Mike, is currently in the 15 percent bracket now and will remain there for a number of years.

Legally, she manages to allocate $10,000 of business profits for the year to Mike instead of herself for that year.

Eileen generates a tax savings of $1,300. Because of her strategic planning, the family will owe $1,500 on this part of the profit instead of $2,800.

Key Observation: Other taxpayers may now face a 35 percent tax bite under the new law. For these taxpayers, the need to evaluate the tax savings through family income splitting is of critical importance.

If Eileen (Illustration 13.1) had reached the top 2003 bracket of 35 percent, her overall savings would have been $2,000 on the $10,000 distribution. In other words, shifting the income means the family would have a $1,500 tax instead of $3,500 on the $10,000.

Clearly, there is a potential to gain measurable savings in income taxes by shifting income from owner-operators to other family members. There are two ways the income can be legitimately shifted to gain these savings.

1. **Pay the family member(s) a salary or fee for services.** Keep records of each individual's work, withhold the appropriate taxes, and issue a W-2.

2. **Share some of the profits.** Make a gift transfer of a part of the business to the family member(s) so they can share in the profits of the operation. The easiest way to accomplish this is to operate as a corporation. A corporation readily facilitates the transfer of ownership of shares back and forth between family members. Another alternative is to use a partnership or LLC in which ownership units may be transferred to other family members.

The FICA Tax

Throughout the years, the added burden of the Social Security tax was not a major factor in evaluating the benefits of income splitting. Today, with the increase of the FICA tax rates, a completely different strategy may be required.

Under the current rate, wages paid to an individual require a 7.65 percent tax to be paid by that individual. In addition, the employer needs to match that payment—bringing the overall cost to a whopping 15.3 percent. For 2003, the FICA tax bite applies to $87,000 in earnings. This limit is raised each year. A small fraction of additional tax continues for Medicare beyond the annual limit.

With an additional 15.3 percent tax, reevaluate the income splitting alternative. Consider Eileen from Illustration 13.1 who is now looking to distribute $10,000 to her 19-year-old son, Mike, to generate healthy tax savings. If she were to make a *salary* payment to Mike, requiring FICA taxes, then the planned savings are drastically reduced. On the other hand, if Eileen would have had to pay the full FICA burden on the $10,000 anyway (because she had not reached the maximum salary level), she would then gain the full benefit of income splitting.

Whether Eileen operates as a sole proprietorship, a corporation, or a partnership has a major significance on the end result. Study each of the following scenarios and find out which will generate your desired tax savings.

Splitting Income as a Sole Proprietorship

If you operate your small business as a sole proprietorship, the easiest way you could distribute income to your teenagers is to simply put them to work. If your teenager works for you for a few hours after school and on weekends on a regular basis, you can

- ◆ deduct the costs of the teenager's salary by keeping adequate time records and being prepared to show that the reasonable amount of paid salary was an ordinary and necessary cost of doing business, and

- ◆ get a special bonus, which is available because a son or daughter employed by a parent's unincorporated business is exempt from Social Security until age 18. When you pay a minor child out of your sole proprietorship, the exemption will apply.

Illustration 13.2

Eileen, operating her business as a sole proprietorship, is in the 28 percent tax bracket, while her son Mike pays 15 percent.

The $10,000 paid to Mike is in the form of salary payments.

Because of the special rule for sole proprietorships dealing with salaries paid to a son or daughter under age 18, Mike's wages are exempt from FICA tax.

Thus, the $1,300 tax savings on the salary payment is not offset by the burden of an added FICA tax.

Q. Does this mean that the only way I could beat the FICA tax dilemma by using my minor children is to pay them through a sole proprietorship?
A. Interestingly, the special exemption also applies to partnerships and LLCs that pay children under age 18 when full ownership is with the parents of those children. For ordinary C or S status corporations, however, the full 15.3 percent Social Security tax will apply.

The Kiddie Tax—When Investment Income Is Involved

Income splitting is a cost effective and perfectly legitimate planning tool for saving income taxes if you play by the rules. However, one rule you must follow involves what is known as the kiddie tax. The kiddie tax primarily applies to investment income over $1,500 earned by minor children. The key is that such income is taxed at the parent's top tax rate rather than the child's. Clearly, this special tax was created by Congress to discourage income splitting between parents and their minor children.

How does the well-known kiddie tax fit into this discussion on family tax planning strategies and income splitting? You probably don't want to go through the time and effort of shifting income to a lower income family member and pay at the same high rate. The following observations will help you plan around the penalty provisions of the kiddie tax:

- ◆ The penalizing provisions of the kiddie tax only apply to children under age 14. You might consider splitting income with older children or else wait until a certain child reaches the prescribed age.

- ◆ Because the special tax applies only to investment income, be careful that you don't distribute too much income in the form of interest, dividends, rents, and profits on sales of property. Remember, once the child receives $1,500 in income from these sources, the tough kiddie tax rules apply.

- ◆ Wages paid to your minor children are not subject to the kiddie tax and could be ignored in an effort to split income.

On the other hand, when you seek to split income by transferring ownership in your business, you'll face an important organizational change, requiring that you carefully play by the following rules:

- ◆ First, you are giving up a legal interest in your business entity; thus, you should ask your attorney to check the legal issues surrounding this action.

- ◆ Second, you are changing the ground rules for tax reporting purposes. The IRS is notified that you are sharing the profits of your business entity with your son, daughter, or another close family member. Your strategic action could create a generous tax savings, and there is nothing the IRS can do if you have the appropriate legal documentation.

You can enjoy significant tax savings by splitting income with other family members, particularly with your own children. Further, there is practically no risk involved when the income splitting comes as the result of salary payments that are properly documented.

> **Key Observation:** The S corporation, like the LLC and partnership, is a convenient device for sharing the ordinary profits of the business with other family members. In many cases, it's as simple as signing over a few shares of stock to those individuals.

Also, S corporations, LLCs and partnerships ordinarily do not pay taxes on generated income. Instead, an information report is filed at the end of the year to identify the individual partners or shareholders who share in the profits. With this information, the IRS is notified of the income amount that is taxable by each of the new owner-participants.

A Checklist of Strategic Family Planning Tips

TRY TO MAKE YOUR GIFT TRANSFERS TAX FREE

If you give your son or daughter a small interest in your business—say some stock or a partnership unit—try to get an independent estimate of the value of the business. This will help you prove the value of the portion given away.

Your child won't have to report this value as income, but you may be required to file a gift tax return if the amount is over $11,000 in any one year. Keep in mind that filing a gift tax return doesn't necessarily mean that you will have to pay any gift taxes. In many cases, such filing is nothing more than a mere formality.

BE CAREFUL ABOUT GIVING YOUR MINOR CHILDREN A PARTNERSHIP OR LLC INTEREST

Children of minor age are not recognized as partners or LLC members unless they are competent enough to manage their own property. If not, the control over the business unit must be given to a fiduciary or custodian for the benefit of the minor. The safest approach is to set up a trust to hold the partnership or interest for that child.

> **Special Note:** When you pass control of a portion of the business to a trust, you must show that you, as a general partner, are not trying to exert ownership rights over the transferred share. The IRS may check the terms of the trust to ensure that this isn't the case.

Your Kind of Partnership Can Make a Difference in Splitting Income

Shifting income with partnership interests usually is not a problem when capital is a material income-producing factor in the business. However, if yours is a service oriented business, such as real estate, insurance, or accounting, then a gift of a partnership interest is inappropriate. The only way the partnership can split the profits with another family member is by that individual actually performing services for the partnership.

Be careful about transferring stock in your S corporation to your minor children. If you wish to transfer stock in your S corporation to your minor-aged child you face problems, unless you have that stock put into a special trust for the benefit of the child. A subchapter S trust can be used for this purpose. Keep in mind, failure to use a qualified trust can cause your S status to be revoked.

Make Sure the Income Splitting of Your S Corporation Has a Sound Basis

The IRS likes to check the method of splitting up profits by S corporations when family members are involved. For these purposes, the term *family* includes spouses, parents, grandparents, children, and trusts for the benefit of such persons.

For example, if one relative of an S corporation shareholder performs substantial services without receiving reasonable pay or interest for capital contributions, a disproportionate share of income will pass through to other shareholders. This will create a significant tax savings because the income will be split with lower bracket shareholders; the IRS may question this.

Most likely, the IRS will recalculate the income to be distributed to each of the shareholders. Then, proper credit is given for the compensation and interest that initially should have been paid to the higher bracket shareholders.

Chapter Summary

If you are the owner of a small business operation and you have a family member who has a smaller income (and a lower tax bracket), you may want to evaluate the possibility of transferring a small portion of the business to him or her. The purpose is to split some of the net income earned and to lower the overall tax bill by having it taxed at a lower rate.

Before you take a step, however, you need to calculate the tax savings by (1) comparing your marginal tax brackets, (2) checking the impact of the FICA tax, and (3) determining if the so-called kiddie tax could thwart your tax saving efforts.

If you determine that you could save taxes by transferring a portion of your business to a family member, you need to determine what kind of business entity would provide the best vehicle for this purpose. That transfer should be accompanied by the least amount of cost and/or gift taxes.

14

Keep Current on the Latest Tax Saving Trends and Ideas

URING THE PAST SEVERAL YEARS, CONGRESS HAS ENACTED A MYRIAD OF IRS code provisions that have been specifically designed to provide additional tax breaks for the small business owner. Many of these provisions are quite revolutionary because they manifest a reform mentality of a Congress that is not afraid to change certain tax law concepts that have been with us forever.

Many of these new loopholes and enhancements have already been discussed throughout other chapters in this book; however, there are other issues that need recognition or further elaboration. It is impossible to define each and every tax saving benefit in the law. But an attempt has been made to identify those that are new along with those that in recent years have sparked a continuing interest among a large segment of small business operators.

Expensing Options: A Welcome Relief for Many

Even the most unsophisticated business owners are keenly aware of the seemingly restrictive rules on depreciation. In short, they lay out money for certain business assets (that have a presumed life expectancy), and the government tells them how much, and when, they will get their coveted tax deduction.

Because of a special tax code section (written for the small business owner) there is instant relief when certain business equipment is purchased. The popular "Section 179" deduction has long been around to grant this special deduction. And now its benefits have been enhanced even further.

The idea behind the Section 179 deduction is simple. As new small business owners learn quickly, this special tax break allows them to write off immediately the *full cost* of certain business assets (equipment, computers, furniture, etc.). This approach could be extremely valuable because the entrepreneur could minimize her or his tax bill right away rather than wait—perhaps as long as seven years—to secure the write-off for the equipment through depreciation.

ENTER THE JOBS AND GROWTH TAX RELIEF RECONCILIATION ACT OF 2003

When President Bush affixed his name to the 2003 tax act, he added a new dimension of opportunities for small business owners who are dismayed by the burden of oppressive taxes. Arguably, for them, the most noteworthy tax break allowed under the new tax act is the unprecedented expansion of the Section 179 deduction—a tax write-off that Congress quadrupled in size.

Year	Amount
2002 (Old Law)	$24,000
2003 (New Law)	$100,000
2005 (New Law)	$100,000*
2006 (New Law)	$100,000*

* Adjusted for inflation

Table 14-1. **Maximum amount that can be expensed for qualifying property placed in service**

Note: The special Section 179 deduction has also been expanded to include off-the-shelf (shrink-wrapped) software placed in service under the new law.

Limitation Alert: The limitation threshold is now set at $400,000 per year. This means that for every dollar you invest over $400,000 in qualifying property you must reduce your Section 179 deduction by one dollar. This means that if you acquire as much as $500,000 in equipment, the special write-off will disappear.

Special Note: The Section 179 deductions are limited to your active business income. However, S corporation owners can add their **W-2** wages, back to the bottom line for purposes of this limitation.

Playing the Depreciation Game: New Bonus Incentive

The ebb and flow of depreciation has for decades reflected the fickle mood of Congress, noted for abiding by the political agenda of the day. At certain times, the lawmakers are lauded for stimulating growth and development by providing generous tax deductions for investing in business property and equipment. Then, like the changing tide, depreciation incentives become inappropriately labeled as "tax shelters" targeted for big business and the very rich." This, of course, provides corrective change with tighter depreciation rules for everyone— as the pendulum swings the other way.

The reality is that readers of this book are probably nowhere near the spheres of big business. Further, most readers would probably not be associated with the "very rich." They are likely to be small, hard-working entrepreneurs seeking to cut their tax bill right now with as much depreciation deduction as the law will allow.

In 2002, the term "bonus depreciation" was reintroduced into the small business owner's vocabulary. In an effort to encourage purchasing of business equipment to stimulate business recovery, the new law allowed an attractive upfront tax write-off for newly acquired property. And now, under the 2003 tax act, an incredible 50 percent depreciation deduction has been introduced—allowing for unprecedented tax savings for business owners in the year that they acquire business property.

Most business assets that you purchase new (other than real estate) after May 5, 2003, and before 2005, will qualify. Typically, the bonus depreciation extends to newly acquired business furniture and equipment, computers, most computer software, machinery, trucks, trailers, etc. Also, certain leasehold improvements in rented commercial property could qualify—providing that those improvements are placed in service more than three years after the building was first placed in service.

Illustration 14.1

On June 30, 2003, with little cash down, Hank bought $100,000 worth of computer equipment for his office—his only major purchases for the year.

The new law allowed Hank to write off as much as $60,000 in 2003. This includes $50,000 in bonus depreciation plus $10,000 for regular depreciation. (Regular first-year depreciation is allowed at 20 percent of the basis that has been reduced by the bonus allowance. In other words, $50,000 x 20 percent = $10,000).

Under the 2003 tax act, Hank could instead elect to write off the entire $100,000 computer immediately as discussed above in the section 179 option. The upfront write-off would be available because Hank did not acquire more than $400,000 in equipment during the year.

However, by not electing section 179, Hank can preserve further depreciation deductions for future use if that meets his business plan.

Special Note: All too often, small business owners jump to write off everything they can just as soon as they can. Remember, a large tax deduction will do you the most good when you are in a higher tax bracket. For example, if Hank were just starting out and expected very little profit in 2003, his tax savings on the $100,000 investment might be minimal or even nonexistent. By contrast, if he expects to level off in a 33 percent bracket (plus state) in the next year, the tax savings that year could be enormous.

Capital Gains Tax Update

For the past several years, the continuing struggle for tax relief has made many investors happy with an attractively low capital gains tax rate of 20 percent. For those in lower tax brackets, the rate has been as low as 8 percent if they held capital assets for more than one year. (Note: Capital assets do not include business inventory and property held for sale to customers.)

Now, thanks to the 2003 tax act, there is even more relief that has been available since May 5, 2003. The top rate is now set at an unheard of 15 percent—and it could be as low as 5 percent for those in the low tax brackets.

THE NEW DIVIDEND INCOME RULES

After much debate, the Bush administration managed to push through a unique tax reduction idea by slashing the tax rate on corporate dividends. Hoping to strengthen the economy, the president repeatedly advocated the need to level the playing field in corporate America by eliminating a phenomenon he called "double taxation." Why, Bush and his administration asked, should the shareholder pay a tax on profits when the corporation has already done so? Well, "double taxation" has not been eliminated entirely under the new law; however, no one can deny it has been minimized greatly.

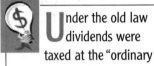

Under the old law dividends were taxed at the "ordinary rates" (10 percent to 35 percent). Starting in 2003, dividends are being taxed at the lower capital gains rates (5 percent to 15 percent).

WHAT'S IN IT FOR THE LITTLE GUY?

It is clear that this major tax reduction on dividends is going to fit nicely in the budget of many investors—particularly those who own stock in major corporations. But what kind of savings will flow to the owners of small corporations (the kinds explained in Chapter 3)? For S corporations there will be no savings because, you will recall, S corporations don't generally pay any tax anyway.

Regular C corporations, however, need to look closer to see if any benefits can be found from the lowered tax on dividends. On the one hand, a regular corporation often pays no tax at all. You learned that it is possible to eliminate corporate tax (or minimize it greatly) by keeping good records of the owner's time and service to the corporation. This effort, presumably, will help justify a substantial (but reasonable) salary that will be deducted from profits, thereby reducing much of the profit. In short, no profit means no dividends and, hence, no tax savings should be expected under the new law.

On the other hand, the regular corporation sometimes does pay some tax, often as part of a well thought out plan designed to retain a small amount of profit and pay some tax in a lower bracket. In that "smaller profit" setting, once again, there rarely is a need to pay any dividends and, likewise, there are no apparent tax benefits to be had under the new law.

Accordingly, the only so-called small corporations that will realize tax benefits under President Bush's plan will be those ordinary corporations that have generated enough profit to require the need to pay dividends to the owner(s).

Illustration 14.2

In 2002, Macko Inc. (a regular corporation) reported a net profit of $200,000 after paying its shareholder, Mack, a salary of $800,000.

After a review by the IRS, it was concluded that $600,000 was the maximum "reasonable" amount of salary that should be allowed. The IRS reclassified the remaining $200,000 as a dividend—taxable to the owner and with no corresponding deduction for the corporation. Thus, on the $200,000, a "double tax" truly existed—a clear-cut penalty to the small business owner in the mind of President Bush.

If the same facts existed under the new law, Mack would have had to pay only $30,000 in tax on the dividend ($200,000 x 15 percent). This would have amounted to a tax saving of $40,000 because he was required to pay $70,000 under the old rules ($200,000 x 35 percent).

Installment Sale Planning Ideas

Although the capital gains tax rates have been slashed drastically, many investors remain resentful about the taxing concept in general. They feel that, over an extended time period, the value of their investment has suffered measurably because of inflationary trends. And, it is still argued, the recapture of their investment in today's dollars is merely a trade-off and shouldn't be taxed at all.

Illustration 14.3

Mabel, a retired widow, owns a piece of rental property, which she purchased 20 years ago to help supplement her retirement needs.

Although her tax basis is only $100,000, she now plans to sell the property for $300,000, a gain of $200,000.

She is advised that her $200,000 gain is subject to the 15 percent capital gains tax and a state tax as well.

Mabel realizes that she stands to lose nearly one-fifth of that gain to taxes, or $40,000.

Now that she has $40,000 (with no adjustment made for depreciation) less to place in fixed yield investments, Mabel is challenged to meet her retirement income goal.

To solve the problem detailed in Illustration 14.3, Mabel could consider arranging an installment sale that would allow her extra leeway by deferring the tax and allowing the capital gains tax to be paid in smaller amounts as the note payment is received. This installment sale approach would keep her money working at full value.

Instead of taking cash in full payment for her property, Mabel agrees to take a down payment and a note requiring monthly payments with 6 percent interest. During the first year, Mabel receives $21,000 toward her principal. In this scenario, she is only required to report $14,000—even though she had a $200,000 profit. This is $21,000 multiplied by two-thirds, which is her profit percentage ($200,000 divided by $300,000 equals 66 percent). Finally, if Mabel is against paying any upfront capital gains tax at all, she might consider a tax-free exchange.

Another Sensible Solution: Tax-Free Exchanges

Frustrated investors are looking more closely at the tax-free exchange alternative as they argue that any capital gains tax at all on their long-term investments is both oppressive and unnecessary.

HOW THE TAX-FREE EXCHANGE ALTERNATIVE WORKS

Generally, you are not required to report a taxable gain when business or investment property is exchanged for "like kind" business or investment property. The term *like kind* refers to the nature or character of the property—not to its grade or quality. To get a better sense of how you can qualify for this definition, take a look at one of the most common types of investment property used with this planning loophole—real estate. When one kind of investment real estate is traded for another, the capital gains tax is fully deferred.

With this broad definition, note the wide variety of real estate exchanges that could qualify for this special treatment. Some examples of tax-free exchanges follow:

- A rental house traded for an apartment building
- Land traded for a building
- Farm land for city lots
- Certain long-term leasehold interests exchanged for outright ownership in realty

---

Illustration 14.4

Instead of selling her rental house outright, Mabel (from Illustration 14.3) decides to trade the property for a real estate investment that generates a higher cash flow. Remember, she needs that extra income stream for her retirement budget.

After locating an attractive small commercial building, she arranges for the potential buyer of the rental house to place a contract on the building and then make a trade with her.

Mabel meets the prescribed deadlines for the property transfers and successfully acquires a new investment property without paying any taxes. The $50,000 in taxes is fully deferred.

Key Observation: If cash is received in a tax-free exchange, you may have to report some capital gain to the extent of the cash received.

Although the capital gains tax may seem confiscatory to many, there are those who will find a relatively attractive tax savings in the maximum capital gains rates prescribed in the current law—a rate that can be as low as 5 percent but cannot exceed 15 percent.

Q. What should higher income earners look for in investments when trying to take advantage of the relatively lower capital gains that cannot exceed 15 percent?

A. One planning idea favors making investments that are geared toward appreciation rather than those that generate high yields such as rents and interest. The latter types of income are taxed at the ordinary rates. On the other hand, a long-term investment in real estate, growth securities, or certain small business corporations can qualify you to take advantage of the lower capital gains rate limited to 15 percent. Surely this is a better option than paying 28 percent, 33 percent, or 35 percent.

Incentive Stock Options: Another Attractive Strategy for Securing the Capital Gain Advantage

Incentive Stock Options (ISOs) are popular devices used by corporations to provide shareholders with special rights to acquire stock. When qualified options are exercised, the employee has no tax liability. If the stock acquired with the option is held for a certain period of time, a major portion of any gain realized will get favorable capital gain treatment. Because of the capital gain advantage under the new tax rates, it is easy to see why the ISOs are becoming increasingly attractive to higher income taxpayers.

A Heads-Up on the Alternative Minimum Tax (AMT)

It can be argued that the most unexpected blind-side tax attack on the American taxpayer is the alternative minimum tax (AMT). All too often, serious-minded business owners, as well as tax professionals, are caught off guard by the AMT—a veritable tax trap for the unwary.

When Congress introduced the AMT, it had but one thing in mind. It wanted to do something about the growing clamor that businesspeople in general were not paying their fair share of taxes. The easy remedy was to put the spotlight on certain tax breaks enjoyed by businesspeople and cause them to pay a special minimum tax for their perceived privileges. The revised taxing procedure, it was felt, would speed up the drive toward equity among all taxpayers.

The idea sounded fair at first. But as time went on, more and more small business owners have become unexpectedly jolted by the harsh reality of the plan. And now, after the 2003 tax act, that reality has become evident as more taxpayers than ever have become subject to the AMT. As the regular income tax rates are being phased down, the pesky AMT burden becomes more likely. This means that the tax reduction, which many taxpayers have been counting on, may suddenly disappear. Some experts predict that, by 2010, the AMT tax will affect one-third of the American taxpayers. That means, of course, a lot of small business owners and investors better pay attention.

Q. Just how do these tax traps work?
A. In general, the tax traps work by identifying certain adjustments and tax

advantages (known as "tax preferences"). These adjustments and preferences are added back to your taxable income and (after allowing a specific exemption) you are assessed a kind of "flat tax" rate. The rate is 26 percent or 28 percent for individuals, depending on the size of your income.

In the past, the small regular corporation needed to be particularly watchful because there were more tax preferences facing them than they cared to remember. Those preferences included bookkeeping procedures such as (1) the way net income was calculated or (2) the method for determining inventory. Preferences like these triggered many a tax trap for the owners of regular corporations who did not plan ahead. Now, the problem of the AMT no longer exists for so-called "small" corporations.

Pass-through entities (such as the S corporation, the LLC, and the partnership) could carry some personal AMT issues for the owners of the business. This is because, like most business income and expenses of a pass-through entity, any tax preferences that exist will ultimately flow through personally to the owner.

Common Tax Preference Items to Look Out for as an Individual Business Owner

It must be emphasized that even though the AMT is a most unwelcome tax trap, those who are affected are still in the minority even after the 2003 tax act. Your income and your tax preferences must be relatively substantial before the AMT will apply. However, the prudent business owner should stay aware of the general rules so there will be no unwelcome surprises as business and earnings grow.

The most common income tax preferences that can trigger the special tax are

- ◆ itemized deductions—including deductions for taxes, medical and miscellaneous expenses,
- ◆ income from the exercise of investment stock options,
- ◆ tax-exempt interest from private activity bonds, and
- ◆ research and experimental costs.

You may not be able to eliminate the AMT entirely from your tax bill. However, you can at least gain a heads-up by being aware of the traps that can create the extra tax liability for you. Further, if it looks like you are approaching the AMT range during a certain year, you may be able to avoid the tax (or soften its blow) with something as simple as changing your accelerated depreciation formula.

Also, you might consider deferring deductions or accelerating income for the purpose of shifting income from one year to another. It is always smart planning to move income from years with a higher tax rate to a year where a lower rate is certain (such as a non-AMT year).

Special Break for Sole Proprietors, LLCs, and S Corporations—Medical Insurance Write-offs

Everyone is aware how tough it is for any individual to get a tax deduction for any kind of medical expenses. Because of the tough threshold requirement, you need to spend a small fortune in medical expenses to be eligible for any benefit whatsoever. Small business owners had found a way around this problem by forming a regular corporation.

In Chapter 3, it was shown that the ordinary corporation could provide a convenient way to beat the threshold requirement and get a full deduction. All that is needed is a corporate medical benefit plan for employees. Forming a corporation had become a popular solution, particularly because of the devastating increase in medical insurance premiums.

Now, as a result of the latest tax law updates, some might not have to go through the cost and effort of forming a corporation to get a write-off for those skyrocketing health insurance premiums (see Chapter 3). Many self-employed individuals are now getting a realistic break for the amount paid for medical insurance for the entire family without incorporating.

The IRS now allows self-employed individuals to deduct a specified percentage of medical insurance premiums paid during the year for themselves, their spouse, and dependents. In 2002 you could deduct 70 percent, and from 2003 on, you can deduct 100 percent. Therefore, since 2002 you don't need a C corporation just to get the full fringe benefit of that important tax write-off for medical insurance premiums.

Passive Loss Relief for Real Estate Professionals

Those small business owner operators and investors who have been involved in real estate are well aware of the restrictive passive loss rules that have been around since 1986. Under these tough rules, anybody who incurs a loss in a business that was deemed to be a *passive activity* is not allowed to write off the loss of that business against other types of income. However, there is an exception allowing up to $25,000 in rental losses when your income is below $150,000.

The passive activities that are subject to the restriction on tax write-offs generally include any business in which the owner operator does not materially participate. Unfortunately, for many real estate investors, rental activities are treated as passive activity regardless of the amount of material participation.

Illustration 14.5

Janet earns $300,000 per year as a planning consultant.

She also owns several rental properties.

Last year, the properties generated a $40,000 loss.

The rental loss is not deductible from her consulting income because it is passive.

Since 1993, special relief from the passive loss rules has been extended to taxpayers who devote more than half their time to the real estate business. Because of the new law, taxpayers can now get a tax write-off for businesses involving real estate activities if they can show that

♦ more than half of the personal services performed are real estate activities and

♦ they perform more than 750 hours of service during the year carrying on a real estate trade or business.

Amortization of Goodwill

This recently revised provision in the law is a welcome tax break to many new business owners. For many years, controversy existed between the IRS and taxpayers over the tax implications of goodwill in a newly acquired business. The IRS's position was clear and unrelenting. Goodwill simply was not allowed as a deduction because the tax law did not allow a deduction for an intangible asset that doesn't have a fixed useful life in a trade or business.

Nearly every individual who purchased a business currently in operation has a goodwill issue for which to be concerned. Whether or not the purchase price was properly allocated on the books of new business owners was the subject of debate by the IRS for many years.

Illustration 14.6

Calvert purchased a printing business for $100,000. Although the seller had been in operation for 35 years and was greatly supported by the community, he agreed that the contract would only show $1,000 as the price to be paid for the goodwill.

The rest of the contract identified $60,000 as the price for the equipment and $39,000 for inventory and supplies—all of which would soon be deducted by Calvert in his new operation.

The IRS determined that $30,000 was the appropriate value of the goodwill and not $1,000.

After reallocating the purchase price, the value of the $30,000 in goodwill needed to be carried on the books indefinitely—never to be written off as a business expense.

Under the current rules, goodwill is now deductible if it was acquired after August 10, 1993. It can now be amortized over 15 years on a straight-line basis.

Assume that Calvert (Illustration 14.6) had bought the business in January 1994. He would be entitled to write off $2,000 in goodwill amortization for 1994 and for each of the next 14 years—or $30,000 divided over the course of the 15 years.

Amortization of Other Intangible Assets

Other intangible assets have long been the source of much controversy and guesswork. Unlike goodwill, many of these assets at least had some sort of finite life and could be amortized accordingly. The problem, however, was determining the appropriate lifespan and separating them from the goodwill that might have been engendered in the transaction.

Fortunately, the current tax law takes away the guesswork. It provides that most intangible assets generally can be amortized on a straight-line basis over a uniform 15-year period. The law also repeals the inconsistent amortization periods of certain intangibles and allows amortization when it wasn't even permitted under the old rules. The following assets are permitted to be amortized under the new uniform procedure over a uniform 15-year period:

- ◆ Workforce in place
- ◆ Information bases, including business books and records, operating systems, and technical and training manuals
- ◆ "Know-how," including secret formulas, designs, patterns, sound recordings, videotapes, and similar items
- ◆ Customer lists, patient and client files
- ◆ Supplier-based intangibles
- ◆ Franchises, trademarks, and trade names
- ◆ Covenants not to compete and similar agreements

Likewise, the new act specifically prohibits the special uniform amortization deduction for several named intangibles. These include the following:

- ◆ Accounts receivable and interests in patents and copyrights
- ◆ Numerous other intangibles not acquired in a business acquisition
- ◆ Interests in land or other business entities

Prove Your Hobby Losses: Pass the Presumption Test

Do you have a side business where you race or train horses? Do you collect and sell coins or stamps? Do you engage in work as an artist or entertainer? It is always interesting to note that when you make money at enterprises such as these, the IRS will tax this income under the usual reporting rules. Further, if you begin to lose money, the IRS may prohibit you from writing off your losses.

As long as there is a profit from your operation, you are able to deduct all the ordinary and necessary expenses of running your business. However, if expenses exceed your income, and an IRS agent succeeds in characterizing your activity as a hobby, you can deduct expenses only up to the amount of your gross income.

WHAT YOU CAN DO

There are two ways to defeat the IRS's allegation that you are merely operating a hobby and not a legitimate business. First, you can pass the *presumption test*. If you can show a profit in three out of the past five consecutive years, then you are safe. The presumption is that you have a legitimate business operation and your losses will probably be allowed. Incidentally, if you breed, race, train, or show horses, you only have to show a profit in two out of seven consecutive years.

However, if you can't pass the presumption test, the burden of proof is greater and you must show that you have

- ◆ spent considerable time and effort trying to make a profit,
- ◆ kept a detailed set of books and records,
- ◆ sought and relied on expert advice,
- ◆ expected the assets to appreciate in value, and
- ◆ proven that losses are common in the early or start-up phase of your type of business.

Remember, do not despair if you are unable to pass the presumption test. Failure to do so will not automatically cause your losses to be disallowed under the law. All it does is shift the burden back to you to prove that you are entitled to the claim.

Key Observation: Many taxpayers have successfully challenged the allegation that they were engaged in hobby activities, even when they had lost money for several years in a row.

Know the Facts When Working with Independent Contractors

Most small business consultants agree that the IRS has been steadily increasing its focus on small businesses that carry their workers as independent contractors on a continuing basis. The new IRS policy is to identify those that have been misclassified. Their overall goal is to set up a tax liability for the unpaid withholding tax and penalties.

If you have never had to administer a regular payroll, you cannot appreciate the extent of the cost and the responsibility for meeting the withholding rules for regular employees. It begins the moment you are placed in the fiduciary role that requires you to withhold and pay the substantial tax costs set by strict federal and state guidelines. These costs include

- ◆ matching FICA taxes that have been withheld,
- ◆ federal and state unemployment taxes,
- ◆ health insurance and certain fringe benefits normally provided to employees, and
- ◆ pension and profit-sharing requirements.

Your first step is to ascertain any existing exposure for unpaid withholding tax. You may want to review your contractual relationship with your independent workers. You will want to make certain that your documents are in order and the requirements for independent contractor status are being met.

Equipped with computerized cross-matching technology, the IRS has recently begun to team up with the state agencies to inspect the subcontract records of small business owner operators.

States such as California, Illinois, Georgia, New York, Michigan, and Texas are actively pursuing this current team effort. To safeguard the independent contractor status of your various workers, you must get acquainted with the state and federal rules to assure compliance. In addition, the IRS has developed the highly successful *Form SS-8*, where a worker who thinks he or she should have been treated as an employee rather than an independent contractor can in essence "turn in" an employer, even years after the working relationship has ended.

If a determination is made that an employer—employee relationship exists, the related tax liability can be retroactively assessed—with penalties. For some, the results can be devastating. If you don't already have a properly thought-out independent contractor's agreement in your files, have one drafted immediately.

For federal purposes, Illustration 14.7 will help you provide the framework for the contract. Additionally, it will alert you to the kind of questions that an examining officer is likely to raise during the course of an audit.

Illustration 14.7

Bryan is a commercial building contractor who subcontracts with Joe, a painter who works on a number of projects with the owners of several office buildings. The IRS auditor asks the following questions:

As a contractor, do you give instructions to the painter about when, where, and how the job is to be done? If Bryan does instruct the painter, this is one strike against him.

- Does the painter work for others? This is a big plus for Bryan if the painter has other clients.
- Does the painter run certain risks of loss in the projects? For example, if Joe has to buy his own materials and pay assistants, the chances are good that he will succeed in proving his independent contractor status.
- Does he set his own hours and days of work?
- Does he publicly advertise as an independent painting contractor? It's a major plus if Joe has his own business cards, stationery, business license, or if he advertises in directories or trade journals.
- Does the commercial contractor reserve the right to fire the painter? Generally, independent contractors cannot be fired as long as they are producing results in accordance with the terms of the contract.
- Is the painter paid "by the job"? Payment made by straight commission or "by the job" is indicative that an independent contractor relationship exists.
- Does he pay for his own insurance?

Clearly, not one of the above criteria can settle the issue of independent contractor status on its own. If viewed together, however, the merit of the overall responses will definitely set the tone for the resulting decision.

Q. Can occasional payments for so-called "casual labor" be treated as independent contractor status in a business?

A. As with any other worker, you need to evaluate the prescribed tests for independent contractor status. Casual employees, unfortunately, are usually subject to enough control to require classification as employees.

Independent contractors cover a wide spectrum of business activities such as the following:

- Accountants

- Health and accident insurance salespeople who are free to solicit business on their own
- Barbers renting chairs in shops
- Church organists
- Commercial fishermen who provide their own equipment and sell to the public
- Consultants
- House-to-house canvassers who are not under the direction and control of a crew manager
- Models who operate on a freelance basis
- Sales agents of a manufacturing company who have an exclusive right to sell in certain territories
- Sales personnel in real estate who have unlimited discretion in their activities and whose work is not supervised
- Tennis professionals who sell their service on the premises of a club—although the club controls the desired results, it does not control how it is to be done
- Writers who furnish a weekly column to a newspaper and have complete control over its content

Under certain circumstances, though, individuals who perform these same services may also be classified as employees.

Tax-Deferred Annuities and Other Formulas to Defer Tax Liability

Ever since the government eliminated real tax shelters in 1986, many small business owners have been busy trying to find other tax-friendly places to put some of their extra cash profits. If they put their money in CDs for example, they have found that not only are they victimized by low interest rates but also that the IRS wants a portion of the earnings as well—perhaps as much as 35 percent.

Say, for example, you put $10,000 into a short-term CD paying 4.5 percent. If your effective tax rate, federal and state, is 33 percent, your true earning on your investment is only 3 percent. If inflation exceeds 3 percent, then obviously you're losing money instead of making it.

With this backdrop, it is easy to see why tax-deferred annuities have become so popular; particularly since their tax-sheltering benefits remain unscathed. However, before you sign up for an investment, know the exact terms.

The following segment is borrowed from a well-known Prentice-Hall Publishing Company publication titled *Executive's Tax Report*. "Tax Deferred Annuities: Getting Beyond the Hype," by Thomas J. Stemmy, is reproduced with permission and has been modified to fit the needs of the small business owner in the current environment. Although interest rates and tax rates have changed since the time of this publication, the general theory remains intact.

How does it (the Tax Deferred Annuity) work? You simply hand over a cash payment (as little as $5,000) to an insurer. You then can choose whether you want a fixed interest rate or a variable rate—similar to choosing a mortgage. The fixed interest rate can be locked in for varying periods from one to ten years. The variable rate fluctuates with the prices of the stock and bond markets. There are several ways to take the money out when you need it. You can make a lump sum withdrawal, or you can get monthly income for life or for a predetermined number of years.

The tax advantages: Tax-deferral is the biggest selling point for an annuity. The tax law says that you don't have to pay taxes on the interest you are earning until you actually withdraw the money (unlike the situation at your local bank where you pay tax on the interest as it accumulates). That can be a big money-saver, especially if your tax rate declines between the time you earn the interest and the time you have to pay on it.

Annuity salespeople like to point out that when you invest in an annuity, not only are you earning interest on your principal and interest on your interest, you're also earning interest on dollars you would have normally paid away in taxes. Below is a comparison of what a $10,000 investment will yield using a tax-deferred annuity (TDA) and without tax-deferral. In both cases a 28 percent tax rate is assumed.

$10,000 at	10 years with a TDA	10 years no TDA	20 years with a TDA	20 years no TDA
8%	$18,340	$17,510	$36,360	$30,650
10%	$21,470	$20,040	$51,240	$ 40,170

There is considerable money to be saved through tax-deferral— especially over longer periods and at higher interest rates. However, don't overlook the fact that this is not tax elimination, just putting off the inevitable. Of course, the idea is that by the time you have to pay tax, you will have retired and your income will have dropped to the point where the tax bite is minimized.

Is it safe? How safe is money that you entrust to an insurer? After all, the newspapers are full of reports of reputable insurers going bust. The answer is that while annuities are a relatively safe investment, your money is only as safe as the company you choose. You should not be shy in asking the insurer its rating. Find out how the insurer fared under the scrutiny of Standard & Poor's, A.M. Best, Moody's, Duff and Phelp's, and the real tough grader, Weiss Research. Also, keep an eye on continuing performance.

Earning potential: While interest paid is comparable to bank rates, it is not unusual for insurers to advertise high starting yields (say 9 percent), then drop to 6 percent or 7 percent after the honeymoon (the initial guarantee period) is over.

Access to your money: Some insurers impose fees as high as 15 percent if you pull money out in the early years. Most will allow you to take out 10 percent of your account value without penalty. Generally speaking, though, your money is always available for an emergency. In addition, the money is readily available to your heirs upon your death—without the delay of probate proceedings. The same cannot be said for a CD at your local bank. However, keep in mind that the IRS generally imposes a 10 percent penalty tax on any withdrawals you make from the annuity before you reach age 59½.

Other Tax-Friendly Investment Options

Voluntary tax-deferral programs, such as tax-deferred annuities, may not be for every small business owner who is looking for a place to invest some of the profits. Accordingly, you may be wondering what other tax-sheltered options are available as an alternative to CDs or other securities that produce a fixed yield. Discuss the following three options with your investment adviser.

MUNICIPAL BONDS

Except in rare cases, municipal bonds still retain their tax-free feature with the federal government. Advice should be sought,

> The best candidates for fixed annuities are conservative investors over 50 years old who are prepared to tie up their funds for 10 years before drawing on them for retirement.

however, on factors such as

- quality or inherent risk of each bond,
- the length of time that you must hold the bond until maturity, and
- the attached commissions and fees.

CORPORATE STOCK

If your business entity is an ordinary corporation, you have a special tax advantage for investments. If you choose to take some of your cash reserves and buy stock in other corporations, in most cases you are permitted to exclude from income 70 percent of the dividends received. This feature becomes particularly attractive when you make the right kind of investment. Ask your broker to recommend the highest yielding and safest stock positions that she or he can find for your account. (See Chapter 3 for this tax-free feature.)

OTHER LONG-TERM INVESTMENT OPTIONS

You can save by focusing your investment dollars on capital appreciation rather than current yield. For one thing, the tax may be lower at capital gains rates. For another, you don't have to pay taxes until the asset is sold—a tax-deferral feature always worthy of merit.

Other equally subtle, tax-saving possibilities exist to put some of your cash reserves to work. Another increasingly popular alternative is tied to the tax-deferral features of certain life insurance products. Ask your insurance consultant how you, as an employer, could recoup your insurance investment, tax free, from the increasing cash surrender value of an insurance policy.

Offer in Compromise: Debt Relief for Many Taxpayers

The government allows some leeway for all those taxpayers who are overwhelmed by their tax obligations to the IRS. Before you begin negotiating with a revenue officer, consider submitting an offer in compromise. For an investigative officer to consider an offer in compromise, at least one of the following criteria must be met:

- **Doubt as to liability.** Doubt exists that the assessed tax is correct.

- **Doubt as to collectivity.** Doubt exists that you can ever pay the full amount of tax owed.

- **Effective tax administration.** You can demonstrate that collection of the tax will create an economic hardship or will be unfair and inequitable.

The ultimate goal is a compromise in the best interest of the government *and* the taxpayer. The offer plan should conform to the goal of achieving collection at the earliest time possible and at the least possible cost to the government.

Many of you burdened with tax debt will find the key in the second bulleted item. Here, you will learn that a relatively small amount of cash is your answer—as long as that amount meets a prescribed minimum (see Illustration 14.8). To further simplify this process, the IRS has made the offer in compromise user-friendly with easy-to-complete forms and a less bureaucratic approach.

REDUCED BUREAUCRACY

The delegation of authority to accept offers is now streamlined, and the IRS will go out of its way to assist. The IRS Code states:

In cases where an offer in compromise appears to be a viable solution to a tax delinquency, the service employee assigned to the case will discuss the compromise alternative with the taxpayer and, when necessary, assist in preparing the required forms. The taxpayer will be responsible for initiating the first specific proposal for compromise.

EASIER FORMS AND FEWER CONTINGENCIES

For many years, taxpayers, particularly business owners, had been plagued with long and complicated "information forms" that needed to be prepared before an offer could even be considered. Now, three forms have been designed to make the job simpler and shorter:

1. Form 656. Offer in Compromise
2. Form 433 A. Collection Information Statement for Individuals
3. Form 433 B. Collection Information Statement for Businesses

Under the most current procedures, a collateral agreement will not be required with every offer as was the case in the past. These side agreements are now being de-emphasized. Thus, taxpayers are not subjected to as many restrictions and contingencies in connection with future activities.

Clearly, the offer in compromise is now becoming a significant planning tool for those small business owners who are financially hard-pressed and whose purpose is to get a fresh start. There are two significant prerequisites.

First, for the IRS to waive a large tax bill, you need to have a current, specified amount of cash. That amount must be no less than the amount of equity you have in everything that you own.

Second, for the deal to work, the IRS also must be satisfied that the amount being offered is not less than the amount that could be generated by the taxpayer's income now and later. In essence, the IRS is ensuring that the amount of upfront money is worth as much now as it will be in future years.

Key Observation: The IRS will closely look at any illegal or questionable maneuvering of assets. This includes the sale of assets to friends and relatives for less than full fair market value or the transfer of assets beyond the reach of the government, like to foreign countries.

Illustration 14.8
Kim, the sole proprietor of a small cleaning service business, owes the IRS $200,000 in back taxes after filing three years of delinquent returns.

The only asset that she owns is her personal residence with a fair market value of $175,000; her mortgage debt is $150,000.

Since it can be ascertained that the net equity of all her assets is $25,000, she will need to come up with at least this amount of cash to make the compromise work.

The value of her present and future income is calculated by taking her monthly income and subtracting her necessary living expenses and multiplying the result by 60 months. Kim's total monthly income is $4,000, and her total expenses are $3,800—the value of her present and future income is $12,000 ($200 multiplied by 60).

In preparing the prescribed offer in compromise forms, Kim sat down to calculate the minimum amount she would have to submit to satisfy her $200,000

obligation to the IRS.
  She made the following computation

A. Her equity in her assets	$25,000
B. The value of her present and future income	$12,000
Total	$37,000

With this information, she set out to borrow $37,000 from a family member and promptly wrote out a check to the IRS, which was then submitted with the offer in compromise.

Look for More Interpretations of the Tax Laws

As more taxpayers challenge the new tax laws, you can be assured of different interpretations that will potentially favor your small business. Keep your eyes and ears open for more tax court rulings that may allow a tax savings for your operation.

Several organizations throughout the country have publications to help you stay abreast of the latest IRS rulings. To learn more about such publications, contact any of the offices listed below.

Helpful Tax Resources

Daily Tax Report (www.bna.com)
The Bureau of National Affairs, Inc. (BNA)
1231 25th St. NW
Washington, DC 20037
(800) 372-1033

The Tax Adviser (www.aicpa.org)
The American Institute of CPAs (AICPA)
1211 Avenue of the Americas
New York, NY 10036-8775
(212) 576-6200

Weekly Alert (www.riahome.com)
Research Institute of America (RIA)
395 Hudson St.
New York, NY 10014
Sales (800) 950-1216

Index